Making Your
FAMILY LIFE
Happy

There is true beauty in a united, happy family. Family life today, however, has come under severe pressures. In some countries persons even ask, "Can the family survive?" This book is published to show that we have every reason for confidence in the success of the family arrangement. It points the reader to the finest source of counsel and guidance for solving family problems. We sincerely hope it will contribute to the happiness of your family.

—The Publishers

Publishers

WATCHTOWER BIBLE AND TRACT SOCIETY
OF NEW YORK, INC.

INTERNATIONAL BIBLE STUDENTS ASSOCIATION

Brooklyn, New York, U.S.A.

This Book Is Published in 77 Languages
Total Books Printed of All Editions:
26,415,000 Copies

Making Your Family Life Happy
English (*fl*-E)

Made in the United States of America

CONTENTS

NOTE: Unless otherwise indicated, Bible quotations in this book are from the modern-language *New World Translation of the Holy Scriptures,* revised edition of 1971.

1

Finding the Key to Family Happiness

MANY human needs for happiness can be satisfied in the family circle. There we may find the things that all of us normally yearn for: to feel needed, to be appreciated, to be loved. A warm family relationship can fill these longings in a wonderful way. It can produce an atmosphere of trust, understanding and compassion. Home then becomes a real haven of rest from outside troubles and turmoil. Children can feel secure and their personalities can blossom out to their full potential.

[2] This is family life as we would like to see it lived. But none of this comes automatically. How can it be attained? Why is it that family life is in such deep trouble today in many parts of the world? What is the key that makes the difference between marital happiness and marital misery, between a family that is warm and united and one that is cold and divided?

[3] If you feel deep concern for the welfare and success of your family, it is with good reason. Describing the importance of the family arrangement, *The World Book Encyclopedia* (1973) says:

1, 2. What fine things can wholesome family life provide? So what questions might be raised?
3. What do the facts of history reveal about the importance of the family?

"Family is the oldest human institution. In many ways it is the most important. It is society's most basic unit. Entire civilizations have survived or disappeared, depending on whether family life was strong or weak."

[4] But how many families today are close-knit with strong bonds of love? How many enjoy the warmth that mutual expressions of kindness, gratitude and generosity bring? How many have learned the truth of the saying, "There is more happiness in giving than there is in receiving"?

[5] Today a very different spirit is spreading throughout the earth. Though prominent in the Western world, it is also penetrating into the Orient and other places where family life has traditionally been quite stable. Included in current views are: 'Do what you want to, and let others look out for themselves.' 'Discipline is old-fashioned; let children choose their own course.' 'Make no judgments of what is right or wrong.' In more and more countries divorce, juvenile delinquency and adult immorality are rising at an alarming rate. Psychologists, psychiatrists, clergymen and other counselors give advice. But instead of fortifying the unity of the family, many advisers condone or even recommend immorality as a means to relieve frustration. The bad harvest from all of this confirms the saying: "Whatever a man is sowing, this he will also reap."

HISTORY SUPPORTS THE FAMILY ARRANGEMENT

[6] The lessons history teaches about the importance of the family merit serious attention. In Part II of *The Story of Civilization,* historian Will

---

4, 5. What undesirable attitudes have you observed in many families?
6. How does what happened in ancient Greece and Rome illustrate the importance of the family?

Durant describes the collapse of the family in ancient Greece, then continues: "The essential cause of the Roman conquest of Greece was the disintegration of Greek civilization from within." He then goes on to show that the strength of Rome was the family, but when the family arrangement broke down because of sexual immorality, the empire went into decline.

⁷ In reality, history confirms the ancient saying, "It does not belong to man who is walking even to direct his step." But it also indicates that there is a source beyond human wisdom that can be looked to for direction, with the result that the family unit prospers. Historians report that, while the Roman Empire decayed, "the family life of the Jews was exemplary, and the little Christian communities were troubling the pleasure-mad pagan world with their piety and decency." (*The Story of Civilization,* Part III, p. 366) What made these families distinctive? They had a different source of guidance, the Bible. To the extent that they applied its counsel as the Word of God, to that extent they enjoyed wholesome, peaceful families. Those results gave the decadent Roman world guilt feelings.

⁸ The sayings quoted in earlier paragraphs are also from the Bible. In that book we find Jesus Christ's words that there is more happiness in giving than in receiving, the inspired apostle Paul's statement that we will reap what we sow, and the declaration of God's prophet Jeremiah that it does not belong to man to direct his steps.

7. Why did certain persons in the Roman Empire enjoy wholesome family life whereas others were experiencing serious problems?
8. When it comes to solving family problems, why does the Bible deserve our attention? (Psalm 119:100-105)

(Acts 20:35; Galatians 6:7; Jeremiah 10:23) These Bible principles have proved true. Jesus also said: "Wisdom is proved righteous by its works." (Matthew 11:19) If the Bible's counsel really works in solving family problems, does it not deserve our respectful attention?

⁹ Today, there are thousands of publications dealing with marriage and family life. Most contain at least some helpful information. Yet family life keeps deteriorating. Something more is needed, something that will give strength to resist the pressures that now threaten the family circle. Natural affection between a husband and wife and between parents and children gives strength. But even this is not proving to be enough to hold many families together when times of crisis arrive. What more is needed?

¹⁰ There needs to be not only a sense of responsibility and devotion to one's mate or children or parents. Along with that, there needs to be an even greater sense of responsibility to the One of whom the Bible speaks as "the Father, to whom every family in heaven and on earth owes its name." That One is the Originator of marriage and family life, mankind's Creator, Jehovah God. —Ephesians 3:14, 15.

GOD'S INTEREST IN THE FAMILY ARRANGEMENT

¹¹ Jehovah God knows mankind's needs and he wants us to be happy, so he gives us counsel on family life. But a grander purpose than this is reflected in his concern for families. The Bible explains what that purpose is. It shows that the

---

9, 10. (a) Why are helpful suggestions and natural affection not enough to enable one to enjoy a happy family life? (b) What else is needed? (Revelation 4:11)

11-13. What is God's purpose regarding the earth and the human family?

earth did not just happen. We did not just happen. Jehovah God created the earth, purposed that it would exist forever and that it would be inhabited forever. The prophet Isaiah recorded: "He the One who firmly established it, who did not create it simply for nothing, . . . formed it even to be inhabited."—Isaiah 45:18.

[12] To accomplish his purpose, God created the first human pair and told them to have a family: "Male and female he created them. Further, God blessed them and God said to them: 'Be fruitful and become many and fill the earth.'" (Genesis 1:27, 28) His purpose further required them and their offspring to obey him and to take care of the earth. Genesis 2:15 states: "Jehovah God proceeded to take the man and settle him in the garden of Eden to cultivate it and to take care of it." Eventually those gardenlike conditions would be extended to embrace the entire globe. Caring for the earth and using its resources would provide the earth-wide family of mankind with unending opportunities to learn and to find satisfaction in using their capabilities.

[13] Now over 4,000,000,000 people are on the earth, but these multitudes do not fulfill Jehovah's purpose for the earth. The majority do not obey him, nor do they care for the earth. Instead, they ruin it, polluting its air, water and soil. In harmony with God's original purpose, he foretold not only that he would stop all of this, but also that he would "bring to ruin those ruining the earth." —Revelation 11:18.

QUESTIONS WE NEED TO FACE

[14] God's purpose regarding the earth and family

14. Why can we be confident that God's purpose regarding family life will not fail?

life will not fail. "My word that goes forth from my mouth . . . will not return to me without results, but it will certainly do that in which I have delighted," he declares. (Isaiah 55:11) God instituted the family arrangement and gave counsel for its operation. His guidelines answer the truly important questions on family life—some of which you may face.

[15] For example: How does a person find a compatible mate for marriage? In marriage, how may agreement be reached on thorny problems? Two minds are better than one, but, after consultation, which one makes the decisions? How can a husband get his wife's respect, and why is this important to him? Why does a wife need her husband's love, and what can she do to assure it?

[16] How do you view children? Some view them as a status symbol, a source of inexpensive labor or old-age insurance; others view them as a burden. But the Bible calls them a blessing. What determines whether they will prove to be that? And when should their training start? Should there be discipline? If so, how much, and what kind? Must there be a generation gap within the family? Can it be closed? Better still, can it be prevented from ever opening up?

[17] Finding the satisfying answers to these questions will do much to assure the happiness of your family life. More than that, it can give you the confidence that there is One of unsurpassed strength, kindness and wisdom to whom you can turn in any time of need, and who can guide your family to never-ending happiness.

15-17. (a) What do you consider to be some of the really important questions on family life? (b) Why is it good to find satisfying answers to these questions?

2

Laying a Fine Foundation for Your Marriage

A HOUSE, a life or a marriage is only as good as the foundation on which it rests. In one of his illustrations Jesus spoke of two men—a wise one who built his house on solid rock and a foolish one who built on sandy soil. When a storm arose, and floodwaters and winds lashed the houses, the one on solid rock stood, but the one on sand fell with a great crash.

[2] Jesus was not teaching people how to build houses. He was emphasizing the need to build their lives on a fine foundation. As God's messenger, he said: "Everyone that hears these sayings of mine and does them" is like the man building on solid rock. But "everyone hearing these sayings of mine and not doing them" is like the one building on sand.—Matthew 7:24-27.

[3] Note that in both cases Jesus shows it is not just a matter of *hearing* wise counsel and *knowing* what to do. What makes the difference between success and failure is the *doing* of what the wise counsel says. "If you know these things, happy you are if you do them."—John 13:17.

[4] This is certainly true of marriage. If we build

1-3. According to Matthew 7:24-27, on what does real success in life depend?
4. What are some things that we can learn from the marriage of the first human pair? (Genesis 2:22–3:19)

11

our marriage on a rocklike foundation, it will stand the stresses of life. But from where does this fine foundation come? From the Creator of marriage, Jehovah God. He started marriage when he brought the first human pair together as husband and wife. Then he gave them wise instructions for their own good. Whether they followed these wise instructions would determine whether they had an everlasting glorious future or no

Can your marriage withstand stormy times?

future at all. Both of them knew God's instructions, but, sadly, they allowed selfishness to prevent them from obeying these guidelines. They chose to ignore the counsel and, as a result, their marriage and their lives collapsed like a storm-lashed house built on sand.

[5] Jehovah God brought that first pair together in marriage, but he does not personally make the marital arrangements for couples today. His wise counsel for happy marriages, however, is still available. It is up to each individual today who contemplates marriage to decide whether he will apply the counsel. God's Word also shows that we can ask him for help in making a wise decision regarding a prospective mate.—James 1:5, 6.

[6] Circumstances, of course, vary considerably in different parts of the earth. In many areas today men and women make their own selection of a marriage mate. But among a considerable part of earth's population the parents work out the marriage, sometimes through a "matchmaker." In some areas a man gets a wife only after paying a "bride price" to her parents, and the size of the price may even put the marriage out of the man's reach. Whatever the circumstances, however, the Bible provides counsel that can help toward the enduring success of a marriage.

KNOW YOURSELF FIRST

[7] What do you want out of marriage? What are your needs—physically, emotionally, spiritually? What are your values, your goals and your meth-

5, 6. What help does God provide for married persons and for those who are contemplating marriage?

7-10. (a) When contemplating marriage, what does a person need to know about himself? How can he find out? (b) What does the Bible say as to the validity of reasons for getting married?

ods of reaching them? To answer these questions you must *know yourself*. This is not as easy as one might think. It takes emotional maturity to examine ourselves, and even then it is not possible to see ourselves as we really are in every detail. The Christian apostle Paul indicated this when he wrote, at 1 Corinthians 4:4: "I am not conscious of anything against myself. Yet by this I am not proved righteous, but he that examines me is Jehovah."

8 On a certain occasion the Creator wanted the man Job to realize some facts that he was failing to discern, and God said to him: "Let me question you, and you inform me." (Job 38:3) Questions can help us to know ourselves and to discover motives. So question yourself about your interest in marriage.

9 Do you want to get married to satisfy physical needs—food, clothing, shelter? Those needs are basic to all of us, as the Bible says: "Having sustenance and covering, we shall be content with these things." And the need for sex? That is also a normal desire. "It is better to marry than to be inflamed with passion." (1 Timothy 6:8; 1 Corinthians 7:9) Is it for companionship? That was a major reason why God established the marriage arrangement. Another was for two persons to cooperate together in work. (Genesis 2:18; 1:26-28) Accomplishing good work is a source of satisfaction and should have its reward: "Every man should eat and indeed drink and see good for all his hard work. It is the gift of God."—Ecclesiastes 3:13.

10 Persons in love have long viewed the heart as a symbol of their feelings. The Bible, however, asks a disturbing question about the heart: "Who

can know it?" (Jeremiah 17:9) Are you sure you know what is in your heart?

[11] Often, physical attraction blinds us to other emotional needs. In seeking a mate, do you give sufficient weight to your need for receiving understanding, kindness and compassion? Basic needs of all of us are: someone to be close to, to confide in, to reveal ourselves to without fear of being hurt; someone who will not shut "the door of his tender compassions" upon us. (1 John 3:17) Can you give all of this to your mate, and will he or she give it to you in return?

[12] Jesus said: "Happy are those conscious of their spiritual need." (Matthew 5:3) What is your spiritual need? Does it relate to seeking a career? Riches? Material possessions? Well, do these pursuits bring inner peace and contentment? Usually they do not. So we need to appreciate that within all persons there is a hunger of the spirit that remains, even after all the physical needs are satisfied. Our spirit hungers for identity—to know who we are, what we are, why we are here, and where we are going. Are you conscious of these spiritual needs, and of the way to meet them?

COMPATIBILITY

[13] If you understand all these needs of body, mind and spirit, do you know whether your prospective mate also understands them? You must not only know your own particular needs for happiness in marriage but also discern the needs of your mate. You surely want your mate

---

11. What basic emotional needs should be satisfied in marriage?
12. Why is the satisfying of physical and emotional needs not sufficient for a happy marriage?
13. For a happy marriage, what must you discern in addition to your own needs?

to be happy also. Unhappiness for one will mean unhappiness for both.

[14] Many marriages end up in unhappiness or divorce on the grounds of incompatibility. Incompatibility is a big word, but its importance in marriage is even bigger. If two persons are not well suited as a team, the going can be difficult. Such a situation brings to mind the provision of the Mosaic law that mercifully prohibited yoking together two animals of different build and strength, because of the hardship it would create. (Deuteronomy 22:10) So, too, with a man and a woman who are not well matched and yet are teamed up in marriage. When mates have different interests, different tastes in friends and recreational activities, and few things in common, the marital bonds come under great strain.

[15] "There is a frustrating of plans where there is no confidential talk," the Bible tells us. (Proverbs 15:22) In considering marriage, have practical matters been discussed? How will the man's work fit into the marriage? It will determine where you live and how much money will be coming in to meet practical needs. Who will handle the budget? Is there need for the wife to work, and is that desirable? What is to be the relationship with in-laws, especially the parents of both parties? How does each one feel about sex, children and the training of children? Does one want to dominate the other, or will kind consideration govern the relationship?

[16] Can all these questions, and others as well, be discussed calmly and logically, and settled in

14. In many marriages, why do mates find that they are incompatible?
15, 16. What are some matters that should be discussed with a prospective marriage mate, and how?

a way that both of you can live with comfortably? Can problems be faced and solved together, and the channel of communication be kept always open? That is the lifeline of a successful marriage.

[17] Greater compatibility usually exists between two persons having similar backgrounds. The book *Aid to Bible Understanding,* page 1114, states about marriage in Bible times:

> "It seems to have been generally customary for a man to look for a wife within the circle of his own relations or tribe. This principle is indicated by Laban's statement to Jacob: 'It is better for me to give [my daughter] to you than for me to give her to another man.' (Gen. 29:19) Especially was this observed among the worshipers of Jehovah, as exemplified by Abraham, who sent to his relatives in his own country to get a wife for his son Isaac rather than to take one from the daughters of the Canaanites among whom he was dwelling. (Gen. 24:3, 4)"

[18] Of course, this does not mean it is advisable for a person today to marry a very close relative, for this could produce genetic problems that might result in defective offspring. But family backgrounds do have much to do with the set of values people have. During childhood and youth a person's conduct and feelings are naturally influenced by the family atmosphere. When the backgrounds of both parties are similar, they usually find it easier to 'grow in the same soil and flourish in the same climate.' However, persons with different backgrounds and origins can also make good adjustments in marriage, especially if both are mature emotionally.

[19] Clearly it is beneficial if you can know some-

17-19. Why do family backgrounds have a bearing on compatibility in marriage?

thing about your prospective mate's family. But also see how he or she relates to the family—to parents and brothers and sisters. How does he or she treat older persons, or get along with young children?

[20] Notwithstanding all the precautions taken, you must still remember this: Compatibility between two persons will never be perfect. Both will have shortcomings. Some they may discern before marriage; some they will become aware of later. What then?

[21] It is not the shortcomings themselves that make marriages fail, but it is how the partner feels about them. Can you see that the good outweighs the flaws, or do you focus on the bad and harp on that? Are you flexible enough to make allowances, just as you need and want allowances to be made for you? The apostle Peter said, "Love covers a multitude of sins." (1 Peter 4:8) Do you have this kind of love for the one you contemplate marrying? If not, it would be better for you not to marry that person.

'I CAN CHANGE HIM'

[22] Do you say, 'I can change him' or 'her,' as the case may be? But with whom are you in love? With the person as he or she is, or as that one will be after your remodeling efforts? It is difficult to change ourselves, much more so to change others. However, powerful truths from God's Word can cause the individual to change himself. A person can "put away the old personality," being made new in the force actuating the mind. (Ephesians

20, 21. In selecting a mate, what view should be taken of individual shortcomings?

22-24. Why is it unwise to marry someone on the basis of his promise to change his ways or with the intent of trying to change the person?

4:22, 23) But be very skeptical of a prospective mate's promise to make a sudden change for you! Though bad habits can be corrected or modified, this may take time, even years. Nor can we ignore the fact that inherited traits and environmental factors have given us specific temperaments and molded us in certain ways to make us distinct individuals. True love can move us to help one another to improve and to overcome weaknesses, but it will not move us to try to force a mate into a new and unnatural mold that crushes his or her personality.

²³ Some have in their minds an image of their ideal, and they try to fit every passing infatuation of theirs into this image. Of course, no one can measure up to an impossible dream, but the infatuated one hangs on tenaciously and tries to force the other person to fulfill it. When this fails, he or she is disillusioned and searches elsewhere to find the imaginary ideal. But such ones never find their ideal. They seek a dream person that does not exist beyond their own fantasies. Persons who think like that are not good marriage material.

²⁴ Perhaps you have had such dreams. Most of us have at certain times in our lives; many young people do. But with increased emotional maturity we realize that such fantasies must be put aside as impractical. In marriage what counts is reality, not mere imagination.

²⁵ Real love is not as blind as many think. It will cover a multitude of shortcomings, but real love is not oblivious to them. It is infatuation, not love, that is blind, refusing to see the problems others can foresee. It even submerges its own

---

25. What is the difference between real love and infatuation?

nagging doubts; but be assured they will surface later on. Close your eyes to unpleasant facts during courtship and you will certainly face them after the wedding. Our natural inclination is to put on our best appearance with someone we hope to please or attract, but in time the full and true picture is seen. Allow yourself that time to see the other person as he or she really is, and be honest in presenting yourself as you actually are. The apostle's exhortation at 1 Corinthians 14:20 could also apply in seeking a mate: "Do not become young children . . . become full-grown in powers of understanding."

COMMITMENTS MADE IN MARRIAGE

[26] One should soberly consider the commitments made in marriage. If the commitment of either person is not strong and solid, the marriage will rest on a shaky foundation. In many parts of the world today, marriages are made and then quickly broken. Often it is because the persons entering the marriage did not view the commitment as morally binding, taking the position instead that 'if it doesn't work out, I'll end it.' Where that viewpoint exists, the marriage is almost doomed from the start and, rather than bringing happiness, generally produces only heartache. The Bible, by contrast, shows that marriage should be a lifelong relationship. God said, of the first pair, that the two "must become one flesh." (Genesis 2:18, 23, 24) For the man there was to be no other woman, and for the woman no other man. God's Son reaffirmed this, saying: "They are no longer two, but one flesh. Therefore, what God has yoked together let no man put apart." Only sexual un-

---

26. According to the Scriptures, how binding is the marriage tie? (Romans 7:2, 3)

faithfulness would be a just basis for breaking the marital bond.—Matthew 19:3-9.

[27] In view of the seriousness of marriage, a woman who wants to be successful in it does well to marry only a man that she can respect—one who is stable and balanced, has sound judgment, is able to handle responsibility and is mature enough to accept helpful criticism. Ask yourself: Will he be a good provider, a good father to any children that may bless the union? Does he have high moral standards so that you can both be firmly resolved to keep the marriage bed honorable and undefiled? Does he manifest humility and modesty or is he proud and opinionated, one who wants to flaunt his headship, who thinks he is always right and is unwilling to reason on matters? By associating with the man for a sufficient time before marriage, these things can be discerned, especially if Bible principles are held to as the standard for judgment.

[28] Similarly, a man who takes the success of his marriage seriously will seek a wife that he can love as his own flesh. She should complement him as a partner in establishing a home. (Genesis 2:18) Being a good homemaker is a demanding career of varied responsibilities. It calls for demonstrating talents as a cook, decorator, economist, mother, teacher, and much more. Her role can be creative and challenging, offering many opportunities for personal growth and fulfillment. A good wife, like a worthwhile husband, is a worker: "She is watching over the goings on of her household, and the bread of laziness she does not eat."—Proverbs 31:27.

27-29. (a) What does a woman do well to look for in a prospective marriage mate? (b) What might a man wisely look for in a prospective marriage mate?

[29] Yes, both do well to give thought to what they see—to evidence of personal cleanliness and orderliness or lack of it; of diligence or, instead, of laziness; of reasonableness and consideration as opposed to stubbornness and egotism; of thriftiness or of wastefulness; of thinking ability that makes for enjoyable conversation and spiritual enrichment as contrasted with mental laziness that makes life a monotonous routine of caring for daily physical needs and little else.

[30] Sincere respect for each other is a key ingredient to a successful marriage. And this also applies to expressions of affection during courtship. Undue familiarity or unbridled passion can cheapen the relationship before the marriage begins. Sexual immorality is not a good foundation on which to begin building a marriage. It betrays a selfish unconcern for the other person's future happiness. The fierce heat of passion that momentarily seems to forge an unbreakable bond can quickly cool and, within weeks or even days, the marriage may turn to ashes.—Compare the account of Amnon's passion for Tamar related at 2 Samuel 13:1-19.

[31] Displays of passion in courtship can sow seeds of doubt that later give rise to uncertainty as to the real motive for the marriage. Was it merely to provide an outlet for passion, or was it to share life with someone who is genuinely appreciated and loved as a person? Lack of self-control before marriage frequently foreshadows lack of it afterward, with resulting infidelity and unhappiness. (Galatians 5:22, 23) Bad memories left by premarital immorality can hinder a smooth emotional adjustment to marriage in its early stages.

30, 31. Why can immoral conduct during courtship hinder one's enjoying a good marriage?

[32] Even more serious, such immorality damages one's relationship with our Creator, whose help we seriously need. "For this is what God wills, the sanctifying of you, that you abstain from fornication; . . . that no one go to the point of harming and encroach upon the rights of his brother [or, reasonably, of one's sister] in this matter . . . So, then, the man that shows disregard is disregarding, not man, but God, who puts his holy spirit in you."—1 Thessalonians 4:3-8.

A ROCK FOUNDATION

[33] Will your household, your family, rest on a foundation of rock or one of sand? In part it depends on the degree of wisdom used when selecting a mate. Beauty and sex are not enough. They do not erase mental and spiritual incompatibility. The counsel in God's Word is what provides a rock foundation in marriage.

[34] The Bible shows that the inner person is more important than the outward appearance. "Charm may be false, and prettiness may be vain," says the inspired proverb, "but the woman that fears Jehovah is the one that procures praise for herself." (Proverbs 31:30) The apostle Peter, a married man, speaks of "the secret person of the heart" and "the quiet and mild spirit" as being "of great value in the eyes of God." (1 Peter 3:4) God 'does not go by a man's outward appearance,' and we can benefit from his example by guarding against being unduly influenced by just the external appearance of a prospective marriage mate. —1 Samuel 16:7.

---

32. How can immoral conduct during courtship affect one's relationship with God?
33, 34. When one is choosing a marriage mate, what qualities do the Scriptures show to be far more important than physical appearance?

[35] Wise King Solomon contemplated life and came to this conclusion: "Fear the true God and keep his commandments. For this is the whole obligation of man." (Ecclesiastes 12:13) The Israelites, in covenant to obey God's law, were specifically commanded not to make marriages with persons who did not share their form of worship, lest it draw them away from the true God. "You must form no marriage alliance with them. Your daughter you must not give to his son, and his daughter you must not take for your son. For he will turn your son from following me, and they will certainly serve other gods."—Deuteronomy 7:3, 4.

[36] For similar reasons the admonition was given to those in God's "new covenant," those in the Christian congregation, to marry only "in the Lord." (Jeremiah 31:31-33; 1 Corinthians 7:39) Rather than manifesting bigotry, this is motivated by wisdom and love. Nothing can give greater strength to marriage ties than mutual devotion to the Creator. If you marry a person who has faith in God and in his Word, and who understands it as you do, then you will have a common authority for counsel. You may not feel this to be vital, but "do not be misled. Bad associations spoil useful habits." (1 Corinthians 15:33) Even within the Christian congregation, however, one does well to be sure that a prospective marriage partner is really a wholehearted servant of God, not one who is trying to live on the fringe of Christianity while leaning heavily toward the attitudes and practices of the world. You cannot walk with God and run with the world.—James 4:4.

35, 36. (a) Why is it important to marry a person who has faith in God and in his Word? (b) To what extent would you expect a prospective mate to be manifesting that faith?

[37] "Who of you that wants to build a tower," Jesus asked, "does not first sit down and calculate the expense, to see if he has enough to complete it? Otherwise, he might lay its foundation but not be able to finish it." (Luke 14:28, 29) The same principle applies to marriage. Since God views marriage as a lifelong union, the selection of a mate should certainly not be rushed. And be sure that you yourself are ready to finish what you have begun. Even courtship is not something to take lightly, like a game. Playing with another's affections is a cruel sport and the emotional bruises and heartache it causes can last a long time.—Proverbs 10:23; 13:12.

[38] Prudent young people considering marriage do well to listen to the counsel of older persons, especially those who have shown that they have your best interests at heart. Job 12:12 reminds us of the value of this by asking: "Is there not wisdom among the aged and understanding in length of days?" Listen to these voices of experience. Above all, "trust in Jehovah with all your heart and do not lean upon your own understanding. In all your ways take notice of him, and he himself will make your paths straight."—Proverbs 3:5, 6.

[39] Many who read these words may already be married. Though to some extent your foundation has already been laid, the Bible can aid you to make adjustments where needed, with rewarding results. Whatever the state of your marriage, it can be enhanced by further reflection on the Creator's counsel on family happiness.

37, 38. (a) Why should one avoid rushing into either courtship or marriage? (b) To whose counsel do those considering marriage do well to listen?
39. How can the Bible be of assistance to persons who are already married?

3

After the Wedding Day

Y OUR wedding is past, and you and your mate are settling down as a new family unit. Is your happiness complete? You are no longer alone but have a companion to confide in, to share your joys and also your problems. Do you find Ecclesiastes 4:9, 10 true in your case?—"Two are better than one, because they have a good reward for their hard work. For if one of them should fall, the other one can raise his partner up. But how will it be with just the one who falls when there is not another to raise him up?" Is your marriage flourishing with this kind of co-operation? It usually takes some time and effort for this happy blending of two lives. But in many marriages, sad to say, it never happens.

² In romantic tales, the problem often is getting the two who are in love together. But then they live happily ever after. In real life, it is living happily afterward, day by day, that presents the true challenge. After the delights of the wedding day comes the daily routine of life: getting up early, going to work, shopping, cooking meals, washing dishes, cleaning the house, and so on.

---

1. How could the kind of cooperation that is described at Ecclesiastes 4:9, 10 benefit one's marriage?
2, 3. (a) What realities of life must be faced after the wedding day? (b) Why is it only reasonable to expect that adjustments will have to be made after a person gets married?

³ The marriage relationship requires adjustments. You both entered into it with at least some expectations and ideals that were not very practical and realistic. When these are not met, some disappointment may come after the first few weeks. But, remember, you have made a big change in your life. You are no longer living alone or with a family that you have been with all your life. You are now with a new person, one you may be discovering that you don't know as well as you thought you did. Your schedule is new, your work may be new, your budget is different, and there are new friends and in-laws to get used to. The success of your marriage and your happiness depend upon your willingness to adjust.

ARE YOU FLEXIBLE?

⁴ Some, because of pride, find it difficult to be flexible. But, as the Bible says, "pride comes before disaster, and arrogance before a fall." To persist in stubbornness can be calamitous. (Proverbs 16:18, *New English Bible*) Jesus recommended that one be willing to bend and yield when he said that if anyone wanted your "inner garment, let your outer garment also go to him," and if someone wanted you to go "for a mile, go with him two miles." Rather than your arguing with someone close to you, the apostle Paul asked: "Why do you not rather let yourselves be wronged?" (Matthew 5:40, 41; 1 Corinthians 6:7) If Christians can go to such extremes to keep peace with others, surely two married persons in love should be able to adjust in order to make a success of their new relationship.

---

4. What Scriptural principles could help a married person to make adjustments? (1 Corinthians 10:24; Philippians 4:5)

[5] There are opportunities everywhere for one to be either happy or unhappy. To which will you be alert? Will you focus on the positive or dwell on the negative? The new wife may think: 'Now that we are married, where is that romantic man who used to take me out to interesting places and spend time with me? He's settled into a rut. He takes me for granted. He's certainly not the man I knew before!' Or does she understand and appreciate that he now works hard to be a good provider for his family? And does this new husband notice that his wife works hard to cook and clean, at times is very tired and does not have as much time to spend trying to look glamorous? Or does he say to himself: 'What's happened to that attractive young lady that I married? She's changed, now that she has her man'?

[6] Both should be mature and realize that neither one has the time or the energy to do all the things that were done before marriage. Now is the time to show flexibility and accept the deeply satisfying responsibility of making marriage work. One person can ruin a marriage, but it takes two to make it work. Making marriage work is an achievement. Achievement implies accomplishing something despite difficulties. When the two of you join in this endeavor, a part of each of you blends into this achievement. This joint effort with a mutual goal ties you together; it binds you close; it makes the two of you one. In time this creates a bond of love surpassing anything felt in anticipation of marriage, and in such unifying happiness it becomes a pleasure to adjust to each other's differences.

---

5. How might one think positively or negatively about one's marriage mate?
6. When husband and wife really work to make their marriage succeed, how does this affect their relationship with each other?

[7] Pride fades as love grows, and there is happiness not only in giving but also in giving in, yielding, when personal preference, and not principle, is involved. It may be the buying of some item for the house, or how to spend a vacation. When concern for the other's happiness is shown, the couple begin to fit the apostle Paul's words: "Keeping an eye, not in personal interest upon just your own matters, but also in personal interest upon those of the others."—Philippians 2:4.

A BALANCED VIEW OF SEX

[8] The Bible is not prudish about sexual intercourse. By poetic figures of speech it shows the ecstasy this should bring to husband and wife; it also emphasizes that sex should be restricted to husband and wife. This passage is found at Proverbs 5:15-21:

"Drink water out of your own cistern, and tricklings out of the midst of your own well. Should your springs be scattered out of doors, your streams of water in the public squares themselves? Let them prove to be for you alone, and not for strangers with you. Let your water source prove to be blessed, and rejoice with the wife of your youth, a lovable hind and a charming mountain goat. Let her own breasts intoxicate you at all times. With her love may you be in an ecstasy constantly. So why should you, my son, be in an ecstasy with a strange woman or embrace the bosom of a foreign woman? For the ways of man are in front of the eyes of Jehovah, and he is contemplating all his tracks."

[9] However, it would be a mistake to overemphasize sex to the point of making it seem that the success of the marriage hinges on the couple's sex life, or that it could compensate for serious

---

7. If decisions must be made, when is it good to be yielding?
8, 9. What is the Scriptural view of marital intimacies?

shortcomings in other areas of the relationship. The flood of sexual material from books, movies and commercials—much of it designed to stir erotic desire—makes sex seem that vital. However, God's Word disagrees, recommending self-control in all areas of life. Even in marriage, throwing off all restraint can lead to practices that cheapen the marital relationship.—Galatians 5:22, 23; Hebrews 13:4.

[10] Adjusting sexually is frequently difficult and may take some time after the wedding. This is usually due to a lack of knowledge and a failure to discern the needs of one's partner. Talking to a respected married friend beforehand may help. Not only are a man and a woman made differently, they also feel differently. Consideration for the woman's need for tenderness is important. But there should be no negative feeling of false modesty or prudery or feeling that sex is somehow shameful. Neither should it become an occasion of conquest, as it does with some men. "Let the husband render to his wife her due," the Bible says, and "let the wife also do likewise to her husband." And in so doing, this Bible principle is appropriate: "Let each one keep seeking, not his own advantage, but that of the other person." If there is such love and desire to please on both sides, a good adjustment will be made.—1 Corinthians 7:3; 10:24.

DISAGREE WITHOUT BEING DISAGREEABLE

[11] No two individuals on earth are exactly the same. Each one is distinctly different. This also

---

10. What are some things to consider that could help a married couple to adjust sexually?

11-13. When there are disagreements, what should we keep in mind so that the differences do not develop into serious rifts?

means that no two people will agree on everything. Most of the disagreements may be trivial, but some of them may be serious. There are homes in which disagreements quickly give rise to shouting, pushing, hitting and things being thrown; one mate or the other may leave for a period of days or weeks, or they may simply quit talking to each other. It is quite possible to disagree without having such a situation develop. How? By facing up to a certain basic truth.

¹² All of us are imperfect, all have flaws, and, despite the best of intentions, weaknesses manifest themselves. The apostle Paul found this to be true in his case: "The good that I wish I do not do, but the bad that I do not wish is what I practice." (Romans 7:19) We have inherited sin from our first parents. Perfection is beyond our powers. So "who can say: 'I have cleansed my heart; I have become pure from my sin'?"—Proverbs 20:9; Psalm 51:5; Romans 5:12.

¹³ We accept our own weaknesses and make excuses for them. Can we not accept and excuse those of our marriage partner? We doubtless will readily acknowledge that we are sinners, but do we become defensive and reluctant to admit to a specific sin? And do we have the insight to understand that this reluctance to admit being in the wrong is typical of people, including our marriage partner, and do we make allowances? "The insight of a man certainly slows down his anger, and it is beauty on his part to pass over transgression," says the inspired proverb. Doubtless you, like just about everyone else, subscribe to the principle of the "golden rule." Jesus stated it in his famous Sermon on the Mount: "All things, therefore, that you want men to do to you, you

also must likewise do to them." Most people give it lip service; few practice it. Its sincere application would solve the problems of human relationships, including marital ones.—Proverbs 19:11; Matthew 7:12.

[14] We each like to be thought of and treated as an individual. When a person compares us unfavorably with someone else, perhaps viewing our qualities or abilities as inferior, how do we react? Generally we feel hurt or resentful. In effect we say, 'But I am *not* that person. I am ME.' Such comparisons are generally not motivating, because we want to be treated in an understanding way.

[15] To illustrate the point: Do you, the husband, express appreciation for the meals that your wife prepares or do you complain that she can't cook like your mother? How do you know how well your mother could cook when she was newly married? Maybe your wife does better than she did. Give your wife a chance to grow into her new duties and become proficient in them. And do you, the wife, complain that your new husband doesn't bring home the salary your father does? What did your father earn when he was newly married? Even that doesn't matter. What matters is the help you give your husband. Do you get up and make breakfast for him before he goes to work, so that he feels you support and appreciate his efforts? Does either one bicker with the other one over the in-laws, or disagree over the friendships to be cultivated or recreation to be engaged in? These and other disagreements may arise. How will you work them out?

14, 15. (a) What can result when one unfavorably compares one's marriage mate with another person? (b) Regarding what matters are such comparisons at times unwisely made?

¹⁶ Some modern psychologists contend that quarrels are useful in resolving difficulties. Their theory is that frustrations build up, generate pressure and finally explode into a violent quarrel. In the heat of such angry exchanges, resentments long held in are blurted out, aired and disposed of—so the theory goes. Until this happens, the frustrations are held within to simmer and stew, and then boil over at a later time. But there is grave danger that such heated outbursts may cause you to say things you do not mean, and wounds may be inflicted that are beyond healing. You may wrong the other person so severely that a barrier is raised that you cannot thereafter breach. As Proverbs 18:19 warns: "A brother who is transgressed against is more than a strong town; and there are contentions that are like the bar of a dwelling tower." The sound counsel found in the Bible is: "Quit before the quarrel breaks out." —Proverbs 17:14, *Revised Standard Version.*

COMMUNICATE!

¹⁷ Far better than letting disagreements build up inside you until they reach explosive proportions, discuss them as they arise. Brooding over a wrong almost always causes it to seem worse than it really is. Discuss it now or forget it. Is it only a passing remark? Let it pass. Does it need discussing? Has your mate done something that distresses you? Don't bluntly condemn; try raising the point in question form, or making a suggestion that will open it up for discussion. For example, you might say: 'Honey, there is something I don't

---

16. What is wrong with the theory that violent quarrels help to resolve difficulties?
17. What might be done to prevent disagreements from building up inside oneself and reaching explosive proportions?

understand. Could you help me?' Then listen. Try to understand the other person's viewpoint. Heed the warning of Proverbs 18:13: "When anyone is replying to a matter before he hears it, that is foolishness on his part and a humiliation." None of us like it when someone jumps to wrong conclusions about us. So, rather than react quickly, endeavor to discern the intent or motive behind the act. Do as Proverbs 20:5 advises: "Counsel in the heart of a man is as deep waters, but the man of discernment is one that will draw it up."

[18] Are you given to moods? A moody person is difficult to live with. Some contend that moods are beyond our control, being governed by chemicals in the brain. Whether that is so or not, feelings are contagious. We may be either cheered up or depressed by those around us. Music can create various kinds of moods in us. Stories also can do this. The thoughts we harbor in our minds affect the way we feel. If you brood on negative things you will be depressed; by an act of will you can force the mind to think positive, optimistic thoughts. Think on them. (Philippians 4:8) If you find this difficult, try some vigorous physical activity—do some hard work, even if it's hoeing weeds or scrubbing a floor; get out and jog or walk in the woods, or, better yet, find something helpful to do for someone else—anything to direct your attention and energies elsewhere. It is far better to nourish a good mood than to nurse a bad one. And it's much more fun, for you and most certainly for your mate!

[19] However, there are times when events grieve you deeply, or severe illness and pain afflict you.

18. What might help us to dispel negative moods?
19. How might one deal understandingly with the moods of one's marriage mate?

Or, in the case of your wife, monthly cycles and pregnancy greatly vary the secretion of powerful hormones that affect the nervous system and the emotions. A woman may be experiencing premenstrual tension without being consciously aware of it. It is a major factor that the husband should keep in mind so that, instead of becoming exasperated, he can show insight. In such special circumstances both husband and wife should recognize what is responsible for any change of temperament and respond in an upbuilding way. "The heart of the wise one causes his mouth to show insight, and to his lips it adds persuasiveness." And, "a true companion is loving all the time, and is a brother that is born for when there is distress."—Proverbs 16:23; 17:17.

[20] Is your marriage partner jealous? It is proper for a person to be jealous of his reputation, and of his marriage also. As adrenaline will start a heart beating again, so jealousy arouses the soul to the defense of something cherished. The opposite of jealousy is indifference, and we should not be indifferent to our marriage.

[21] But there is another kind of jealousy, one induced by insecurity and fed by the imagination. Such unreasoning, overly possessive jealousy turns the marriage into an unpleasant prison where trust and true love cannot survive. "Love is not jealous" in such a manner, and obsessive jealousy "is rottenness to the bones."—1 Corinthians 13:4; Proverbs 14:30.

[22] If your mate has just cause for feeling insecure due to jealousy, remove that cause immediately. If there is no real cause, do all in your power to build up the confidence of the jealous

20-22. (a) Why is undue jealousy to be avoided? (b) What might be done to give one's marriage mate a feeling of security?

one, by words and even more importantly by your
actions. Reach for the heart!

[23] Can outsiders be of help in resolving disagreements between married persons? Possibly, but they
should not be called in unless both marriage
partners agree to it. First, "plead your own cause
with your fellowman, and do not reveal the confidential talk of another." (Proverbs 25:9) There
is a special risk in asking in-laws to arbitrate.
They are not likely to be impartial. Wisely, the
Bible says: "A man will leave his father and his
mother and he must stick to his wife." (Genesis
2:24) The same applies to the wife in relation to
her parents and her husband. Instead of asking
parents or in-laws to arbitrate, taking sides with
one mate against the other, the husband and wife
should stick together, recognizing their problems
as ones that they share and that need to be worked
out together. To appeal to outsiders without the
other partner's consent demeans both in the eyes
of others. If you will communicate openly, honestly
and lovingly, there is no reason why you should
not be able to solve your problems yourselves.
Other mature persons may be consulted for advice,
but the solution ultimately rests with you and
your mate.

[24] "Do not be conceited or think too highly of
yourself," the apostle Paul advises. (Romans 12:3,
New English Bible) He then adds: "In showing
honor to one another take the lead." (Romans
12:10) Sometimes when our pride is injured it
helps to reflect that we are not really so big.
Certainly we are not big in comparison to the

---

23. What might beneficially be considered when a person is
inclined to seek the help of outsiders in resolving marital problems?
24, 25. What might a person do if pride interferes with the
resolving of a marriage problem?

earth, and the earth is itself small in the solar system, which, in turn, is tiny in the universe. In Jehovah's eyes "all the nations are as something nonexistent . . . as nothing and an unreality they have been accounted to him." (Isaiah 40:17) Such thoughts help to keep things in perspective, to see that disagreements may not involve such vital things after all.

²⁵ At times a sense of humor may also help us to keep from taking ourselves too seriously. To be able to laugh at yourself is a mark of maturity and smooths out many rough spots in life.

"CAST YOUR BREAD UPON THE WATERS"

²⁶ What if your mate does not respond to your efforts to solve differences peacefully? Follow the Bible's advice: "Return evil for evil to no one." Jesus is our model to copy: "When he was being reviled, he did not go reviling in return." The common practice among persons is to return like for like. But if you take this course you let others shape you, make you what you are. Actually, they make you what *they* are. To let this happen is to deny yourself, what you stand for, the principles you hold dear. Instead, copy Jesus, who holds true to what he is, unchanged by the weaknesses of those around him: "If we are unfaithful, he remains faithful, for he cannot deny himself." —Romans 12:17; 1 Peter 2:23; 2 Timothy 2:13.

²⁷ If you are strong enough to stop a cycle of evil with good, you may start a cycle of good. "An answer, when mild, turns away rage." (Proverbs 15:1) A mild answer does not come from weakness but springs from strength, and your mate will

---

26, 27. What Bible principles should be applied when one's marriage mate does not respond to efforts to settle differences peacefully, and why?

sense this. Since so many return like for like, your breakthrough with goodness may switch the cycle from evil to good. Certain scriptures indicate this. "The one freely watering others will himself also be freely watered." "With the measure that you are measuring out, they will measure out to you in return." "Cast your bread upon the waters, for you will find it after many days." (Proverbs 11:25; Luke 6:38; Ecclesiastes 11:1, *Revised Standard Version*) It may take time for your goodness to bring in a harvest of good from your mate. You don't sow seed one day and reap on the next. Nevertheless, "whatever a man is sowing, this he will also reap; . . . So let us not give up in doing what is fine, for in due season we shall reap if we do not tire out."—Galatians 6:7-9.

[28] Here are some scriptures and questions for married couples to consider:

Proverbs 14:29: "He that is slow to anger is abundant in discernment, but one that is impatient is exalting foolishness." If you give yourself time to think, do you not often discover that there's no good cause to be angry?

Proverbs 17:27: "Anyone holding back his sayings is possessed of knowledge, and a man of discernment is cool of spirit." Do you keep your spirit cool, and hold back words that would make your mate's spirit hot?

Proverbs 25:11: "As apples of gold in silver carvings is a word spoken at the right time for it." The word that is right at one time may be wrong for another time. Are you perceptive as to what is the right word at the right time?

Proverbs 12:18: "There exists the one speaking thoughtlessly as with the stabs of a sword, but the tongue of the wise ones is a healing." Before you speak, do you stop and think what effect your words will have on your mate?

Proverbs 10:19: "In the abundance of words there does not fail to be transgression, but the one keeping his lips in check is acting discreetly." Sometimes when upset we say more than we mean, and we are sorry afterwards. Do you guard against this?

Proverbs 20:3: "It is a glory for a man to desist from disputing, but everyone foolish will burst out in it." It takes two to argue. Are you mature enough to be the one to stop?

Proverbs 10:12: "Hatred is what stirs up contentions, but love covers over even all transgressions." Do you continually rehash old disputes, or do you love your mate enough to put them behind you?

Proverbs 14:9, "New English Bible": "A fool is too arrogant to make amends; upright men know what reconciliation means." Are you too proud to make concessions and seek peace in your marriage?

Proverbs 26:20: "Where there is no wood the fire goes out." Can you stop arguing, or must you have the last word?

Ephesians 4:26: "Let the sun not set with you in a provoked state." Do you dwell on differences and thereby prolong the misery for both yourself and your mate?

²⁹ Wise counsel benefits only when it is put into practice. Try it out. Similarly, be willing to try the suggestion your mate makes. See if it works. Who is to blame if something goes wrong? That's not important. What is important is how things can be made right. Be flexible, air differences, talk them out, and don't take yourself too seriously. Communicate! If you 'love your mate as you do yourself,' it should not be too difficult to adjust to the marriage relationship and to make it a happy one.—Matthew 19:19.

---

29. What are some basics to keep in mind when seeking to maintain a happy marriage?

4

A Husband Who Gains Deep Respect

R ESPECT is not gained by merely ordering someone to respect you. You must earn respect by how you speak and act and by what you are.

[2] This is illustrated in the case of Christ Jesus. He gained respect as a teacher by his manner of teaching. After his Sermon on the Mount "the effect was that the crowds were astounded at his way of teaching." What earned him this respect? His relying on God's word the Bible instead of the opinions of other men. His sole authority was Jehovah God and His word of truth. Jesus gained respect from both friend and foe, by earning it. —Matthew 7:28, 29; 15:1-9; John 7:32, 45, 46.

[3] "The wife should have deep respect for her husband," is the instruction given at Ephesians 5:33. But the husband should be diligent to merit this respect; otherwise, it will be very difficult for his wife to comply with this instruction. How can a husband fulfill his role as outlined in the Bible so as to gain such respect?

1, 2. How is respect gained, and how is this well illustrated in the case of Jesus Christ?
3. What obligation does Ephesians 5:33 put upon a wife, and what does this require of a husband?

BY EXERCISING PROPER HEADSHIP

⁴ The Bible assigns the husband to a position of headship in the marriage arrangement, saying: "Let wives be in subjection to their husbands as to the Lord, because a husband is head of his wife as the Christ also is head of the congregation, he being a savior of this body. In fact, as the congregation is in subjection to the Christ, so let wives also be to their husbands in everything." (Ephesians 5:22-24) Will this arrangement really contribute to happiness in the household? Some women speak out against what they describe as male chauvinism, that is, a vainglorious or exaggerated view that some men have toward their position in relation to women. But let us say at the outset that the teachings of the Bible do not endorse such male chauvinism.

⁵ The Bible emphasizes the fact that, not only the woman, but also the man is under headship. Turning to the Bible book of 1 Corinthians, chapter 11, verse 3, we find that the apostle Paul wrote these words to the congregation at Corinth: "I want you to know that the head of every man is the Christ; in turn the head of a woman is the man; in turn the head of the Christ is God." Man has Christ as his head, and it is from God and Christ as examples and teachers that you, the husband, are to learn how headship is to be exercised.

⁶ Jehovah's headship over Christ was exercised in loving-kindness, and Christ's response was, "To do your will, O my God, I have delighted." (Psalm

---

4. What place does the Bible assign to a husband?
5. What should a husband recognize about headship, and whose examples should he follow?
6. What can husbands learn about headship from Jehovah God and Jesus Christ?

40:8; Hebrews 10:7) Jesus Christ's headship, too, is loving. To those who would become his disciples he said: "I am mild-tempered and lowly in heart, and you will find refreshment for your souls." (Matthew 11:29) Those who are members of his congregation, which the Scriptures liken to a bride, have indeed found such refreshment under his headship. He has not exploited them, but has been self-sacrificing in his love. This also is the kind of headship the husband is to exercise over his wife: "Husbands, continue loving your wives, just as the Christ also loved the congregation and delivered up himself for it . . . In this way husbands ought to be loving their wives as their own bodies. He who loves his wife loves himself, for no man ever hated his own flesh; but he feeds and cherishes it, as the Christ also does the congregation . . . let each one of you individually so love his wife as he does himself; on the other hand, the wife should have deep respect for her husband." (Ephesians 5:25-29, 33) If you set the example of submission to the headship of Christ, it will not be a difficult thing—in fact, it can be a pleasure—for your wife to have deep respect for your headship as her husband.

[7] The great problem is that due to imperfection and inborn selfishness there are times when a husband, while wanting to be respected as the head of the family, fails to show the needed love and consideration for his wife. Often a wife will say that she doesn't feel loved by her husband, that his only concern is his own pleasure and satisfaction. Also, some wives complain that their husbands are domineering. Perhaps this has re-

---

7, 8. Mention some of the ways in which some husbands fail to exercise proper headship.

sulted from the wife's attempts to usurp his headship, with his resisting such usurpation. Or, the
man may have grown up in an environment where
many husbands are arrogant and domineering.
Regardless of the cause, such abuse of headship
gains the respect of no one.

⁸ On the other hand, instead of abusing headship, some husbands abdicate it. They pass all
the decision-making over to their wives. Or, while
telling the wife 'not to rush them,' they pro-
crastinate so much that family interests suffer.
They may not be lazy or idle physically, but if
they shy away from mental effort the results can
be the same as those described in Proverbs 24:33,
34: " 'A little sleep, a little slumber, a little folding
of the hands to rest,' and poverty will come upon
you like a robber, and want like an armed man."
—*Revised Standard Version.*

⁹ You will gain respect from your wife if you
show yourself steady and strong and able to make
decisions. But that does not mean that no one else
in the household is to be consulted or that your
wife's opinion is not to be given serious consideration just because it does not happen to agree
with yours. Early in the Bible record we read
about a serious problem in the household of Abraham and Sarah, involving their son Isaac and the
son of their servant girl Hagar. Sarah recommended a solution that did not coincide with
Abraham's feelings on the matter. But God told
Abraham: "Listen to her voice."—Genesis 21:9-12.

¹⁰ We are not to conclude from this that a husband should always accede to his wife's wishes.
But it can be beneficial to discuss with her those

9, 10. When making decisions that affect the family, whose
views should a husband consider?

decisions that affect the family, encouraging her to express her thoughts and feelings freely. Keep open the lines of communication, always be approachable, and weigh carefully her preferences in the decisions you make. Never be bossy or tyrannical in exercising headship, but manifest humility. You are not perfect, you will make mistakes, and when you do, you will want your wife's understanding. When those situations arise, the wife whose husband is humble will find it easier to respect his headship than will one whose mate is proud.

BY BEING A GOOD PROVIDER

[11] It is the husband's responsibility to provide the material necessities of life for his family. First Timothy 5:8 shows this: "Certainly if anyone does not provide for those who are his own, and especially for those who are members of his household, he has disowned the faith and is worse than a person without faith." To live today, in many lands, it takes a great deal of money, and you as the husband must make the decisions that govern how this need will be met. You will probably find that, in addition to bringing home the money you earn, you will need to work out with your wife a budget that you both understand. This simply means having an arrangement for controlled spending. It will help you to live within your means, and it can do much to avoid the kind of arguments that sometimes arise when the money runs out before payday.

[12] Although in most cases it is the husband

11, 12. (a) What is the husband's responsibility as to providing material necessities of life? (b) How is it really by joint effort that such provisions are made?

who brings in the money for the family's support, it should not be forgotten that it is earned by a joint effort. If you, the husband, think you are doing this by yourself, then just stop and figure out what it would cost you to hire a purchasing agent, a cook, a dishwasher, a housekeeper, a decorator, a nursemaid, and so forth. Normally, your wife saves this expense by doing the work, which is, of course, her share as the marital partner. And if she keeps a lot of the records of home expenses you can add "accountant" to the preceding list. Very true is Proverbs 18:22: "Has one found a good wife? One has found a good thing."

[13] In providing materially, there is the ever-present danger—for you and for your wife—of slipping into a materialistic outlook and approach to life. Few things can 'eat away' at the foundation of family happiness as much as this does. "We have brought nothing into the world, and neither can we carry anything out," says the Bible writer Paul. "So, having sustenance and covering, we shall be content with these things. However, those who are determined to be rich fall into temptation and a snare and many senseless and hurtful desires, which plunge men into destruction and ruin. For the love of money is a root of all sorts of injurious things, and by reaching out for this love some have been led astray from the faith and have stabbed themselves all over with many pains." No matter what possessions a materialistic way of life may bring, it can never compensate for the pain of seeing family relations weaken and break

13. When it comes to material things, what outlook should married couples avoid, and how can this benefit them?

down. The material gain is far outweighed by the spiritual and emotional loss.—1 Timothy 6:7-10.

[14] Materialism is *love* of material things, not merely having material possessions. A person can be poor and materialistic, or rich and spiritually minded. It depends on where his heart is. Jesus said: "Stop storing up for yourselves treasures upon the earth, where moth and rust consume, and where thieves break in and steal. Rather, store up for yourselves treasures in heaven, where neither moth nor rust consumes, and where thieves do not break in and steal. For where your treasure is, there your heart will be also."—Matthew 6:19-21.

[15] A husband who is a good provider of material needs will reflect on such Scriptural admonition, and besides providing the things needful in a material way will devote time to making spiritual provisions for his family. What's the good of spending so much time at secular work to obtain the material things of life that you do not have sufficient time and energy left to build up your household in a spiritual way? In order to have the wisdom to cope successfully with the problems of life, time must be spent to build into the family a strong devotion to right principles. Making place in your life for reading and talking together about God's Word can do that, as will united prayer. As family head, it is up to you, the husband, to take the lead in this. The cost in time and effort will be far outweighed by the benefits. God's promise will not fail: "In all your ways take

---

14. What determines whether material things are too important in a person's life?
15, 16. Besides caring well for material needs, what else should a husband do in order to maintain a happy family?

notice of him, and he himself will make your paths straight."—Proverbs 3:6.

¹⁶ A husband who looks to the Creator to direct his steps appreciates the balance in the counsel found at Ecclesiastes 7:12: "Wisdom is for a protection the same as money is for a protection; but the advantage of knowledge is that wisdom itself preserves alive its owners." So, as a good provider, he works hard to supply the physical needs of his household. Nevertheless, he rests his hope, "not on uncertain riches, but on God." He sets an example in putting the primary emphasis on spiritual interests, in order that both he and his wife may "get a firm hold on the real life." (1 Timothy 6:17-19) The efforts of a husband to make such provisions, both physically and spiritually, will win the respect of a God-fearing wife.

BY SHOWING HER HONOR

¹⁷ The apostle Peter talks to husbands about their wives and tells them to be "assigning them honor as to a weaker vessel, the feminine one." (1 Peter 3:7) In this same verse Peter points out that you, the husband who dwells with your wife, should be assigning her this honor "according to knowledge."

¹⁸ This certainly applies in sexual relations. Much frigidity in wives is due to husbands who are ignorant of a woman's physical and emotional makeup. "Let the husband render to his wife her due," but let it be done 'according to knowledge, assigning her honor as to a weaker vessel,' counsels God's Word. (1 Corinthians 7:3) If you truly 'assign her honor,' you will not be harsh and demanding, insisting on satisfying your own passions

17-19. How might the Bible's counsel to assign "honor" to a wife be applied in connection with sexual relations?

even when she may be very tired or during difficult times of the month. (Compare Leviticus 20:18.) And when you do have relations, you will not be so intent on your own pleasure that you ignore her needs. In this area of life a woman usually responds slower than a man. She has a special need for tenderness and affection. In telling the husband to "render to his wife her due," the Bible puts the emphasis on giving, not getting.

[19] That kind of giving, of course, is to be reserved for one's own marriage mate. True, many men today have "affairs" with other women. But in the end what do they gain? They simply undermine the happiness of their own home. They fail to 'assign honor' to their wives, and so they provide no basis for their wives to respect them. More than that, they dishonor marriage itself, an arrangement that originated with God. In view of all the heartache this brings, it is understandable why Hebrews 13:4 urges: "Let marriage be honorable among all, and the marriage bed be without defilement, for God will judge fornicators and adulterers."

[20] Showing honor to one's wife does not end with sexual relations. In other matters, too, the husband who is truly respected shows that he has high regard for his wife. It is not that he puts her on a pedestal and becomes her slave. Rather, it is as we read earlier from Ephesians 5:28: "Husbands ought to be loving their wives as their own bodies. He who loves his wife loves himself." A man who does this surely is not going to treat his wife as if she were an inferior person. At mealtimes he certainly wouldn't feel that his body

20. As indicated at Ephesians 5:28, in what other ways should a wife be shown honor?

Little things mean a lot

merited all the choice portions, with hers getting only the leftovers—not if he loves her 'as his own body.' Rather than being self-centered about his own appearance, he will be as much or more concerned about his wife's, doing what he can to help her feel content about her clothes. A man does not hit himself when he fails to do as well as he might like. Nor will a Christian husband do that to his wife just because she sometimes falls short of his expectations. Very much to the contrary, if anyone should treat her harshly he would loyally come to her aid. He loves her as he does his own body.

[21] While appreciating the areas in which your needs are alike, you also need to understand the psychological differences between the two of you if you are going to 'assign honor' to your wife. Basically, women like to work under a ceiling of authority, provided that it is exercised properly. This is the way Jehovah God created them. Woman was made to be 'a helper for the man, as a complement of him.' (Genesis 2:18) But if the supervision is too close, if there is no room to take initiative and use her own abilities, a woman can begin to feel that the enjoyment is being squeezed out of her life, and resentment may develop.

[22] Another vital factor that needs attention is the woman's natural desire to feel needed. A helpful husband is appreciated by most wives, but one who simply pushes his wife aside and takes over may find that he has done more harm than good. You do much to win your wife's loyalty if you are kind and appreciative and let her know that she is needed, that you hold her in honor, that you are working as a team, that it is "we" and "our," not "I" and "you" or "mine" and "yours." Do you really let your wife know how much you appreciate and need her? You don't do it by paying her a salary; you must show it in other ways.

21, 22. How can a husband help his wife to find enjoyment in fulfilling her role?

APPRECIATE HER FEMININE QUALITIES

[23] A woman psychologist wrote: "Basically, women *feel* while men *think*." By itself, one trait is not better than the other; they simply are different. We do not care for people who are unfeeling; neither do we like thoughtless persons. Obviously, women have the capacity both to feel and to think, and the same is true of men. But, generally speaking, a woman's emotions more readily come to the fore, while a man is usually more inclined to try to subdue emotion in favor of what he considers a logical approach to matters. Though exceptions, of course, are found, this is another difference that makes husband and wife complements of each other. Along with her basically more emotional makeup, her strong interest in people often causes her to talk more than the man. And she needs someone to return the talk. This is where many husbands fall short.

[24] Do you talk to your wife? Not just about your work, but hers as well? Are you interested in it, and do you show her that you are? How was her day? What happened with the children? Don't come home and ask, 'What's for dinner?' and, after eating it, hide your head behind a newspaper and grunt in response to her endeavors to talk. Be interested in your wife, her thoughts, her activities, her feelings about things. Encourage her in her projects, commend her in her accomplishments. If she is complimented on what she does, she may start doing other tasks she may have neglected. Criticism can be a subtle poison and a

---

23. Generally speaking, how do men and women differ as to emotions?
24. Why is it important for a husband to listen to his wife and to talk with her?

depressant, but genuine praise given where deserved is a curative and a stimulant that makes the spirit soar!—Proverbs 12:18; 16:24.

[25] Do you bring her an occasional gift? Not necessarily an expensive one—perhaps just a small item that says, 'I was thinking of you.' And do you do this, not necessarily for a specific occasion, but just spontaneously, for no other reason than that you wanted to? Pleasant surprises are always a delight. Are you not pleased when she surprises you by preparing some special dish that you like? Return surprise for surprise, and please her. Small remembrances, prompted by love, mean more than expensive gifts routinely—perhaps even begrudgingly—offered out of a sense of duty. "God loves a cheerful giver." (2 Corinthians 9:7) So do wives. Even if meals aren't special, remember, "Better is a dish of vegetables where there is love than a manger-fed bull and hatred along with it."—Proverbs 15:17.

[26] The most important giving is the giving of yourself—your time, your energies, your attention and your thoughts, especially those closest to your heart. Many men find this difficult. To make expressions of endearment may seem to them like foolish sentimentality and somehow unmanly. But if you love your wife, you will keep in mind how much a look, a touch, a word can hold for a woman. But the absence of these can do much to make her feel cross, weary, unhappy. So, follow the example recorded in the Bible's Song of Solomon. Expressing regard and affection for others is good for the one making the expressions. People are irresistibly drawn to warm people. And what is

25, 26. (a) What message does a gift convey to a wife? (b) What kind of giving is most important to her?

a warm person? A person who reveals his feelings and enthusiasm to those he cares about. Such warmth is contagious; it will be returned to the giver.—Song of Solomon 1:2, 15; Luke 6:38.

[27] Husband, ask yourself: Is my headship easy for my wife to respect? Do I love her as I do myself? Or am I interested primarily in just my own satisfaction and wants? How much do I consider her needs? Before I make family decisions, do I listen to her views and consider her desires? Are my decisions made with her welfare in view? Do I assign her honor as a more fragile vessel, the feminine one? Do I communicate with her, and open up my heart to her?

[28] You will not be able to measure up perfectly. But if you put forth a consistent and humble effort, you can be confident that this will go a long way toward making you become a husband who gains your wife's deep respect and God's approval.

27, 28. (a) What might a husband ask himself, to determine whether he is exercising headship in a proper way? (b) Why is it good to be concerned about this matter?

5

A Wife Who Is Dearly Loved

ONE woman complained to another, 'I know my husband loves me, but he never says it. Oh, occasionally, if I drag it out of him, but it would mean so much more if he would say it without my prompting.'

[2] The other woman replied, 'I know. That's the way men are. One time I asked my husband if he loved me, and he said, "I married you, didn't I? I support you, I live with you; I wouldn't do it if I didn't love you." '

[3] She paused a moment, then continued: 'However, something very touching happened the other evening. During the day I was cleaning in his study, and in one of his desk drawers I saw a snapshot. It was one I had shown him from an old family album of mine. It was of me in a bathing suit when I was seven years old. He had pulled it out of the album and put it in his desk drawer.'

[4] She smiled as she recalled this, then looked at her friend. 'I confronted him with it that evening when he got home from work. He took the snapshot in his hand and smiled, and said, "I cherish this little girl." Then he laid it down and took my face in both his hands and said, "I cherish

1-4. What complaint do women at times make about husbands' assuring them of their love?

54

what she became, too." And he kissed me very tenderly. It brought tears to my eyes.'

⁵ A wife who knows that she is very dear to her husband feels warm and safe inside. God's Word counsels men to have such love for their wives. "Husbands ought to be loving their wives as their own bodies. He who loves his wife loves himself, for no man ever hated his own flesh; but he feeds and cherishes it, . . . the two will become one flesh." (Ephesians 5:28, 29, 31) As we have already discussed, the wife is to have deep respect for her husband, but the husband ought to conduct himself in such a way as to earn that respect. The same holds true in this case where your husband is counseled to love and cherish you: Conduct yourself in ways that impel him to do so from the heart.

DO YOU GIVE SUPPORT?

⁶ For a wife to be dearly loved, more is required than mere submission under her husband's headship. He could have a horse or a dog that is well trained and submissive to him. Adam had animals with him in the garden of Eden, and they were in subjection to him. But he was still alone as to his kind. He needed an intelligent human companion that would be a complement of him and a helper to work with him: "It is not good for the man to continue by himself," Jehovah God said. "I am going to make a helper for him, as a complement of him."—Genesis 2:18.

⁷ What a husband needs is a wife who not only

---

5. To be dearly loved by her husband, how should a wife conduct herself?

6, 7. (a) At Genesis 2:18, for what role did Jehovah say that he made woman? (b) In order for a wife to be a real helper to her husband, what is required of her?

loves and respects him but also is a real helper, supporting him in the decisions that he makes. This is not difficult when decisions are mutually agreed upon after discussion together. But it may not be so easy if you were not consulted or if you do not happen to agree. In such a case could you loyally support your husband— do your best to make his decision work, provided it is not some illegal or unscriptural activity? Or would you be inclined to hold back stubbornly, hoping to see him fail so you could say, 'I told you so'? If he sees you working hard for the success of the project, in spite of your misgivings, don't you think such loyal support on your part will cause him to love you all the more?

[8] Above all, don't try to usurp his headship! If you succeed, you won't like him; and he won't like you or himself. Maybe he does not take the lead as he should. Can you encourage him to do so? Do you express appreciation for any effort he makes at taking the lead? Do you cooperate with and encourage him when he does show some initiative, or do you tell him that he is wrong, that his plan won't work? Sometimes a wife must share the blame if her husband doesn't take the lead—for example, if she belittles his ideas or opposes his efforts, or gives the I-told-you-it-wouldn't-work response when the project falls short of perfection. This can eventually produce an uncertain, indecisive husband. On the other hand, your loyalty and support, your trust and confidence in him, will strengthen him and contribute to his success.

---

8. How can a wife encourage her husband to exercise proper headship?

"A capable wife . . . her value is far more than that of corals." —Proverbs 31:10.

"A CAPABLE WIFE"

[9] To be a wife who is dearly loved, you also need to care well for your responsibilities in the home. Of such a woman the Bible says: "Her value is far more than that of corals." (Proverbs 31:10) Are you such a wife? Do you want to be?

[10] When discussing the activities of a "capable wife," the book of Proverbs reports: "She also gets up while it is still night, and gives food to her household." (Proverbs 31:15) Many young women start off married life with a handicap because their mothers did not teach them how to cook; but they can learn. And a wise woman will learn how to do it well! Cooking is an art. When a meal is prepared well, it not only fills the stomach but also brings response from the heart.

[11] There is much that can be learned about preparing food. It is beneficial to become informed on the basics of nutrition so that you can safeguard the health of your family. But simply setting nutritious food before your husband is not necessarily going to win his praise. The Bible tells us that Isaac's wife, Rebekah, knew how to prepare food in a "tasty" manner, in such a way that her husband was fond of it. (Genesis 27:14) Many wives could benefit from her example.

[12] In some parts of the world women go to the market every morning to get the things that they need for the day. Elsewhere, they shop perhaps once a week and keep the perishables refrigerated. Whatever the case, a man cannot help but appreciate a wife who uses household funds carefully, and who respects the family budget. If she

---

9. What does Proverbs 31:10 say about a capable wife?
10, 11. How might a wife show that she fits the description of Proverbs 31:15?
12. What could be included in a woman's acting in harmony with Proverbs 31:14?

learns how to identify food and clothing that are of good quality, and knows their value, she will not always buy the first thing she sees. Rather, as Proverbs 31:14 says: "She has proved to be like the ships of a merchant. From far away she brings in her food."

[13] That conscientious concern about her work also needs to be reflected in the condition of her home. In commenting further on what identifies a wife as being capable, Proverbs 31:27 says: "She is watching over the goings on of her household, and the bread of laziness she does not eat." Making it a habit to sleep late, spending excessive amounts of time in idle chatter with the neighbors—these are not for her. Although illness or unforeseen circumstances may at times cause her to fall behind in her housework, her home will generally be neat and clean. Her husband can be confident that, if friends come to visit, he will not be embarrassed by the appearance of their home.

[14] Most women do not need to be told that it is also important to give attention to their personal appearance, but some do need a reminder. It is not easy to feel affection for someone whose appearance shows that she doesn't think much of herself. The Bible recommends that women "adorn themselves in well-arranged dress, with modesty and soundness of mind." But it also counsels against putting too much emphasis on hairstyling, jewelry and expensive garments that draw undue attention to the wearer.—1 Timothy 2:9.

[15] Of far greater value than such attire is the disposition of the one who wears it. The apostle

---

13. According to Proverbs 31:27, what can be expected from a capable wife in connection with care of the home?
14, 15. What is the Bible's counsel to women respecting attire and adornment?

Peter tells Christian wives that a "quiet and mild spirit . . . is of great value in the eyes of God." (1 Peter 3:3, 4) And Proverbs, when enumerating the traits of a capable wife, adds that "her hands she has thrust out to the poor one" and that "the law of loving-kindness is upon her tongue." She is neither selfish nor "catty" but is generous and kind. (Proverbs 31:20, 26) "Charm may be false," the description continues, "and prettiness may be vain; but the woman that fears Jehovah is the one that procures praise for herself."—Proverbs 31:30.

¹⁶ Yes, such a woman will be dearly loved by any husband who shares the viewpoint of the Creator. He will feel about his wife as expressed by the writer of Proverbs: "There are many daughters that have shown capableness, but you— you have ascended above them all." (Proverbs 31:28, 29) And without a lot of prompting, he will be moved to let his wife know that he feels that way.

YOUR VIEW OF SEX MAKES A DIFFERENCE

¹⁷ Unsatisfactory sexual relations are at the root of many marriage problems. In some cases this is due to the husband's lack of consideration and understanding of his wife's physical and emotional needs, and in other cases it is the wife's failure to share physically or emotionally in the experience with her husband. The sex act, willingly and warmly participated in by both husband and wife, should be an intimate expression of the love that they feel for each other.

¹⁸ Frigidity in a wife may be due to a lack of

16. How will an appreciative husband feel about such a wife?
17, 18. How can the wife's view of sex affect how her husband feels about her?

consideration by her husband, but a wife's indifference also hurts the husband, and a show of distaste may kill his potency or even cause him to feel attracted to someone else. If the wife merely submits, with a couldn't-care-less attitude, the husband may interpret this as evidence that his wife doesn't care for him. Emotions rule sexual responsiveness, and if the wife is unresponsive she may need to review her own attitude toward sex.

[19] The Bible counsels both husband and wife not to "be depriving each other of it." God's Word makes no allowance for using sex as a means of punishing one's mate or expressing resentment, as in a wife's denying it to her husband for weeks or even months. Just as he is to "render to his wife her due," she is also to "do likewise to her husband." (1 Corinthians 7:3-5) This does not mean that a wife should be expected to submit to some abnormal act that she finds morally repugnant, and a husband who loves and respects his wife would not require her to do so. "Love . . . does not behave indecently." (1 Corinthians 13:4, 5) It should not be necessary to ask someone outside the marriage union to rule on the propriety or impropriety of the couple's conduct. The Bible, at 1 Corinthians 6:9-11, clearly enumerates practices forbidden to worshipers of Jehovah God: fornication, adultery, homosexuality. (Compare also Leviticus 18:1-23.) Some modern liberals practicing a "new morality"—actually immorality—clamor for acceptance of some of these forbidden sexual acts, while others who are very

---

19. (a) How does the Bible show that it would be wrong to deny sex relations to one's mate for extended periods of time? (b) Why should it not be necessary to ask persons outside the marriage union to rule on the propriety of a couple's conduct in matters of sex?

conservative would add to these prohibitions. The Bible gives the balanced view. Generally speaking, if all the other relationships in the marriage are good, if there are love, respect, good communication and understanding, then sex will seldom be a problem.

[20] A wife who is dearly loved does not use sex for bargaining purposes. Certainly not all wives bargain with sex, but some do. In ways that may be subtle they use sex to gain concessions from their husbands. What is the result? Well, you don't feel tender affection for the person who sells you a dress, do you? Neither does a husband feel tender affection for a wife who trades sex for concessions from him. The woman who does it may gain materially, but she loses emotionally and spiritually.

THE WEEPERS, THE NAGGERS

[21] Samson was a strong man, but he could not bear up under the pressure of women who used weeping or nagging to get their way. On one occasion he was confronted with a siege of weeping from the woman who was to become his wife. As recorded at Judges 14:16, 17, she "began to weep over him and to say: 'You only hate me, you do, and you do not love me. There was a riddle that you propounded to the sons of my people, but to me you have not told it.' At this he said to her: 'Why, to my own father and my own mother I have not told it, and ought I to tell it to you?'" Samson's appeal to logic did not work. It seldom does when emotions are running high. "She kept

20. If a wife uses sex for bargaining purposes, what is the result?
21-23. As illustrated in the case of Samson, how can a woman's weeping and nagging destroy happiness?

weeping over him the seven days that the banquet continued for them, and it came about on the seventh day that finally he told her, because she had pressured him. Then she told the riddle to the sons of her people."

²² Do not think your husband does not love you just because he does not always give you your own way. Samson's wife-to-be accused him of not loving her, but in actuality she was the one who did not love him. She brought pressure to bear on him until he could stand it no longer. When he did tell her his riddle, she immediately betrayed his confidence, racing off to tell his secret to his enemies. In the end, she became the wife of another man.

²³ Later, Samson became attracted to another woman, Delilah by name. She may have been physically attractive, but did she prove to be a woman that he could dearly love? In order to wheedle from Samson information that she could use for selfish advantage, Delilah used nagging as her tool. The account says: "It came about that because she pressured him with her words all the time and kept urging him, his soul got to be impatient to the point of dying." The final results were tragic.—Judges 16:16.

²⁴ Weeping and nagging are not wise. They are damaging to a marriage. They alienate a husband. The Bible warns against such practices, as in the following scriptures quoted from *The New English Bible:* "He who harps on something breaks up friendship." "A nagging wife is like water dripping endlessly." "Better to live alone in the desert than

---

24-27. (a) What does the book of Proverbs say about the effect of a wife's nagging? (b) Why does it single out women for this counsel? (c) What is most likely to move a husband to want to do nice things for his wife?

The women
in Samson's life

with a nagging and ill-tempered wife." "Endless dripping on a rainy day—that is what a nagging wife is like. As well try to control the wind as to control her! As well try to pick up oil in one's fingers!"—Proverbs 17:9; 19:13; 21:19; 27:15, 16.

²⁵ Why do the Scriptures single out the wife for this counsel? Probably because women are generally more emotional and more inclined to give vent to their feelings, especially when they are disturbed about something. Also, they may feel it is the only weapon they have. As head of the house a husband may arbitrarily have his way, so the wife may feel that she must resort to putting on emotional pressure. You, the wife, should not indulge in such tactics, and your husband should not make you feel forced to do so.

²⁶ True, there may be times when you don't feel well, and perhaps you find yourself giving way to tears, even when you wish you wouldn't. But that is quite different from employing highly charged emotional scenes simply to get your own way.

²⁷ If they truly love their wives, most husbands will favor their wives more than they do themselves, where personal preferences are involved. Please your husband, and he will likely seek opportunities to please you.

"A TIME TO KEEP QUIET AND A TIME TO SPEAK"

²⁸ Many wives complain, 'My husband never talks to me.' The fault may be his. However, many times a husband would like to talk with his wife, but she doesn't make it easy for him. In what

---

28-35. (a) Describe conversation habits that might make it difficult for a husband to converse with his wife. (b) What can be done to improve conversation between husband and wife?

way? Not all women are alike. But ask yourself whether you fit one of these descriptions:

29 The first is a woman who has no trouble at all in talking with other women in the neighborhood. But what is her style? When the other woman stops for a breath, she breaks in. She may throw in a couple of questions, or she may take off on an entirely different subject. Soon the one interrupted cuts in and again carries the conversational ball for a while. Neither one seems to mind this conversational free-for-all.

30 Now her husband comes home, and he has some news to tell. As he enters the door, he starts out, 'You'll never guess what happened at work . . .' He never gets any farther. She interrupts him with, 'How did you get that spot on your coat? Be careful where you walk. I just cleaned the floor.' He may hesitate to take up his story again.

31 Or, perhaps they are conversing with friends and he is relating an experience, but he leaves out some of the details or doesn't get them all exactly right. His wife cuts in, first to correct the flaws, then to round out the story. Before long he takes a deep breath and says, 'Why don't you tell it?'

32 Another woman is the kind who encourages her husband to talk. Trying to appear casual, but bursting with curiosity, she asks: 'Where were you?' 'Who was there?' 'What happened?' Not the routine things of life, but those that seem to be more confidential, are the ones that intrigue her. She pieces together the bits of information that she can glean and fills in the gaps with a bit of imagination. Perhaps some of it is information her husband should not have divulged. Other things may have been appropriate for discussion

with his wife, but they were told in confidence. If she now talks about this to others, the confidence has been broken. "Do not reveal the confidential talk of another," Proverbs 25:9 warns. But if she did, it may cause problems. How free will he feel about talking to her in the future?

[33] Yet a third kind of woman is not much of a talker herself. She knows how to do the necessary work around the house, but she seldom has more than a few words to say. Anyone who tries to converse with her has to do all the talking. Perhaps she is timid, or it may be that she had little opportunity for education when she was a child. Regardless of the cause, efforts at conversation with her fall flat.

[34] But changes can be made. The art of conversation can be learned. If a woman does, not only her housework, but also worthwhile reading and kind deeds for other people, she will have upbuilding things to share with her mate. And successful conversation requires sharing. It also requires respect—enough respect to let him finish what he is saying, to let him say it in his own way, and to know when there is a confidence to be kept. As Ecclesiastes 3:7 says, there is "a time to keep quiet and a time to speak."

[35] Therefore, instead of complaining that your husband seldom talks to you, why not try to make it a pleasure for him to do so? Be interested in the things that he does. Listen intently when he speaks. Let your response reflect the warm love and deep respect that you have for him. Be sure that the things you talk most about are of a positive, upbuilding nature. You may soon find that conversation is a pleasure to both of you.

"WON WITHOUT A WORD"

[36] At times, actions speak louder than words, and especially so with husbands who are not fellow believers of God's Word. Of them the apostle Peter said: "They may be won without a word through the conduct of their wives, because of having been eyewitnesses of your chaste conduct together with deep respect." (1 Peter 3:1, 2) Many a nonbelieving husband has complained that his wife is always "preaching" to him, and he resents it. In contrast, others have become believers by seeing the change that the truth of God's Word has made in their wives. People are often more impressed by seeing a sermon than by hearing one.

[37] When you speak to your unbelieving mate, "let your utterance be always with graciousness," in good taste, or "seasoned with salt," as the scripture puts it. There is a time to speak. "As apples of gold in silver carvings is a word spoken at the right time for it," the Bible says. Is he discouraged about something? Maybe things went wrong at work. A few understanding words might be treasured by him right now. "Pleasant sayings are . . . sweet to the soul and a healing to the bones." (Colossians 4:6; Proverbs 25:11; 16:24) Or, depending on the situation, just to slip your hand into his may say it all: I understand, I'm on your side, I'll help if I can.

[38] Even though he is not one with you in your faith, God's Word shows that you are still to be in subjection to him. Your good conduct may in time win him over, so that he shares your faith. What a happy day that would be! And if that time

36-38. What are some ways to reach the heart of a mate who is not a fellow believer?

comes, he will realize that he has more reasons to love you than he ever knew. Because your devotion, coupled with firmness for what you knew to be right, will have helped him to lay hold of "the real life."—1 Corinthians 7:13-16; 1 Timothy 6:19.

³⁹ The Scriptures encourage Christian wives, whether their husbands are believers or non-believers, "to love their husbands, to love their children, to be sound in mind, chaste, workers at home, good, subjecting themselves to their own husbands, so that the word of God may not be spoken of abusively."—Titus 2:4, 5.

⁴⁰ If you, the wife, do this to the best of your ability, you will be dearly loved, not only by your husband, but also by Jehovah God.

39, 40. What qualities, listed at Titus 2:4, 5, make a wife precious, not only to her husband, but also to Jehovah?

6

Love, "a Perfect Bond of Union"

'WHY can't we ever have supper on time?' her husband snapped, tired of waiting and worn out after a hard day's work.

² 'Quit complaining. It's almost ready,' she flared back. Her day had not been easy either.

³ 'But you're *always* late. Why can't you *ever* be on time?'

⁴ 'That's not true!' she shouted. 'But if you'd try to take care of the children someday, you wouldn't complain so much. After all, they're your children too!'

⁵ So between husband and wife this molehill grows into a mountain, leaving both of them angry and not speaking to each other. Each one reacts to the other's responses, until both are hurt and resentful, and their evening is spoiled. Either one could have prevented this buildup. As it was, both were too involved with their own feelings and oblivious to those of their mate. Frayed nerves snapped.

⁶ Such problems can arise in many areas. They might involve money. Or the husband might feel that his wife is overly possessive, not letting him enjoy the company of other people. She might

---

1-6. (a) What can happen when marriage mates are too involved with their own feelings? (b) Heeding what Scriptural principles could prevent the buildup of a serious argument?

feel neglected and taken for granted. Tension could exist because of a big problem or several minor ones. Whatever the case may be, our concern right now is how the situation is to be approached. Either mate can stop the buildup toward trouble by being willing to 'turn the other cheek,' being willing not to "return evil for evil," but instead 'conquering the evil with good.' (Matthew 5:39; Romans 12:17, 21) To be able to do this takes restraint and maturity. It takes Christian love.

WHAT LOVE REALLY MEANS

7 Jehovah God inspired a definition of love, in terms of what it is and what it is not, at 1 Corinthians 13:4-8: "Love is long-suffering and kind. Love is not jealous, it does not brag, does not get puffed up, does not behave indecently, does not look for its own interests, does not become provoked. It does not keep account of the injury. It does not rejoice over unrighteousness, but rejoices with the truth. It bears all things, believes all things, hopes all things, endures all things. Love never fails."

8 Love may be based on many things—physical attraction, family relationship or mutual enjoyment of another's companionship. But the Bible shows that, to be of true value, love must go beyond affection or mutual attraction and be governed by what is for the highest good of the loved one. That kind of love can even call for reproving or disciplining, as a parent might do with a child, or as Jehovah God does with his worshipers. (Hebrews 12:6) Feelings and emotion are there, of course, but they are not allowed to overrule

7-9. (a) How is love described at 1 Corinthians 13:4-8? (b) What kind of love is this?

wise judgment or right principles in dealing with others. That kind of love moves one to treat all according to fine principles of consideration and fairness.

⁹ To appreciate more fully how it can benefit our family life, let us consider in greater detail the definition given at 1 Corinthians 13:4-8.

¹⁰ *"Love is long-suffering and kind."* Are you long-suffering with your mate? Even when a situation tends to provoke, and perhaps unfair accusations are made, do you exercise restraint? Jehovah is long-suffering with all of us, and 'the kindly quality of God is trying to lead persons to repentance.' Both long-suffering and kindness are fruits of God's spirit.—Romans 2:4; Galatians 5:22.

¹¹ Love does not approve of wrongdoing, but it is not "picky." It is not impatient. It takes into account extenuating circumstances. (1 Peter 4:8; Psalm 103:14; 130:3, 4) And even in serious matters it is ready to extend forgiveness. The apostle Peter doubtless thought he was being long-suffering when he asked Jesus: "How many times is my brother to sin against me and am I to forgive him? Up to seven times?" Jesus' answer was: "Not, Up to seven times, but, Up to seventy-seven times." (Matthew 18:21, 22; Luke 17:3, 4) Love forgives repeatedly, and is kind endlessly. Are you?

¹² *"Love is not jealous."* It is difficult to live with a mate who is jealous without genuine cause. Such jealousy is suspicious, overly possessive. It is childish and restrains the other person from being natural and friendly around others. Happiness is

10, 11. What would we expect from a marriage mate who is long-suffering and kind?

12, 13. How may jealousy manifest itself, and why should efforts be made to keep it in check?

in giving freely, not in meeting a jealous demand.

¹³ "Who can stand before jealousy?" the Bible asks. It is one of the works of the imperfect flesh. (Proverbs 27:4; Galatians 5:19, 20) Are you able to detect in yourself any signs of the kind of jealousy that results from a feeling of insecurity and is fed by imagination? It usually is not hard to see the flaws in another person, but we profit more when we examine ourselves. "Where jealousy and contentiousness are, there disorder and every vile thing are." (James 3:16) Jealousy can wreck a marriage. Your mate will not be held safe by jealous restrictions, but by loving attention, by consideration and trust.

¹⁴ Love *"does not brag, does not get puffed up."* It is true that many persons do it, but few people like to hear bragging. In fact, it may embarrass anyone who knows the braggart well. While some persons brag by talking about themselves in a boastful manner, others accomplish the same thing in another way. They criticize and run down others, and by comparison this tends to elevate them above their victims. So, a person may elevate himself by lowering others. Belittling one's mate is really a way of bragging about oneself.

¹⁵ Have you ever found yourself talking in public about the shortcomings of your mate? How do you think it made your mate feel? What if you had been the one whose flaws were being exposed? How would you have felt? Loved? No, love "does not brag," either by praising self or by belittling others. When talking about your mate, be upbuilding; it will strengthen the bond between you. And as for what is said about yourself, apply the wise

14, 15. (a) How does bragging show a lack of love? (b) Instead of belittling one's mate, what should one do?

counsel found at Proverbs 27:2: "Let another praise you, and not your own mouth; a stranger, and not your own lips."—*Revised Standard Version*.

[16] Love "*does not behave indecently.*" There are many things that are strikingly indecent, such as adultery, drunkenness and fits of anger. (Romans 13:13) In contrast with love, all of these cause damage to the marriage bond. Rudeness, vulgar speech and actions, as well as neglecting personal cleanliness, all show a lack of human decency. How careful are you to avoid being offensive to your mate in this regard? Do you treat him or her with consideration, good manners, respect? All these things contribute to a marriage that is happy, one that endures.

[17] Love "*does not look for its own interests, does not become provoked.*" It is not self-centered. How much better it would have been if the couple mentioned at the beginning of this chapter had been that way. The husband would not have snapped at his wife because supper was late, and she would not have flared back. If the wife had discerned that his irritation was partly because he was tired, instead of being provoked she might have replied: 'Supper is almost ready. You must have had a hard day at work. Let me give you a cool glass of juice to drink while I put things on the table.' Or if the husband had been more understanding, not thinking only of himself, he might have asked whether there was anything that he could do to help.

---

16. What are some indecencies that a loving person would avoid?
17. How can quarrels be avoided by a person not looking for his own interests?

[18] Are you easily provoked by something your mate says or does, or do you try to discern the intent behind the word or act? Maybe it was innocent, only thoughtlessness, and no offense was intended. If you have love, 'the sun won't set with you in a provoked state.' (Ephesians 4:26) What if your mate felt frustrated, and really did mean to say or do something that would hurt? Can't you wait until tempers cool and discuss it then? Approaching the situation with the best interests of both at heart will help you to say the right thing. "The heart of the wise one causes his mouth to show insight." "The one covering over transgression is seeking love," not stirring up more strife. (Proverbs 16:23; 17:9) By fighting down the impulse to continue an argument and prove yourself right, you can gain a victory in favor of love.

[19] Real love *"does not rejoice over unrighteousness, but rejoices with the truth."* It does not think it clever to deceive one's mate—whether as to the use of one's time, the spending of money, or in one's associations. It does not employ half-truths in order to appear righteous. Dishonesty destroys confidence. For there to be genuine love, both of you must rejoice to communicate the truth.

TRUE LOVE HAS STRENGTH AND ENDURANCE

[20] *"It bears all things, believes all things, hopes all things, endures all things."* It bears up under the stresses and strains put upon it in marriage, while the two in this close relationship learn to be flexible and adjust to each other. It believes all

---

18. How can love prevent one from becoming provoked?
19. (a) What might be included in 'rejoicing over unrighteousness'? (b) Why should this be avoided?
20. How does love (a) 'bear all things'? (b) 'believe all things'? (c) 'hope all things'? (d) 'endure all things'?

the counsel set out in God's Word and earnestly applies it, even when circumstances seem to be unfavorable. And, while not being gullible in dealing with persons who resort to dishonesty, it is not unduly suspicious. Rather, it displays trust. Moreover, it hopes for the best. Such hope is based on the confident assurance that applying Bible counsel will yield the best results possible. Thus, love can be positive, optimistic and forward looking. Also, it is not fickle, nor is it a passing infatuation. Real love endures, facing up to problems when the going is hard. It has staying power. It is strong; but with all its strength, it is kind, gentle, yielding, easy to live with.

[21] Such *"love never fails."* If hard times press the couple into financial straits, what happens? Instead of thinking about finding an easier life somewhere else, the wife who has such love loyally sticks with her mate, seeking to economize and perhaps to supplement her husband's income. (Proverbs 31:18, 24) But what if the wife becomes afflicted with an illness that is prolonged for years? The husband who has this kind of love does all he can to provide the care she needs, to help out with work at home that she is not now able to do, and to provide assurance of his continued devotion. God himself sets the example in this regard. No matter what the circumstances into which his faithful servants come, 'nothing can separate them from God's love.'—Romans 8:38, 39.

[22] What problems could prevail over a love like that? Does your marriage have it? Do you personally practice it?

21, 22. What are some circumstances illustrating that love never fails?

MAKING LOVE GROW

²³ Love, like a muscle, is strengthened by use. On the other hand, love, like faith, is dead without works. Words and acts, motivated by feelings deep within us, are said to come from the heart, representing our inner motivation. "Out of the abundance of the heart the mouth speaks. The good man out of his good treasure sends out good things." But if the feelings within us are wicked, "out of the heart come wicked reasonings, murders, adulteries, fornications, thieveries, false testimonies, blasphemies."—Matthew 12:34, 35; 15: 19; James 2:14-17.

²⁴ What thoughts and feelings do you cultivate in your heart? If you daily meditate on the ways in which God has shown love, and seek to imitate his example, fine motivations will be strengthened. The more you exercise this love, the more you act and speak in harmony with it, the more deeply inscribed it will become on your heart. Daily practice of it in little things will make such love habitual. Then, when occasional big issues arise, this love will be there, strongly entrenched, to help you to cope with them.—Luke 16:10.

²⁵ Do you notice something commendable in your mate? Give voice to it! Do you have an impulse to do a kindness? Obey that impulse! We must show love in order to reap it. Practicing these things will bring you and your mate closer, make the two of you one, make the love between you grow.

²⁶ To increase love, share it. The first man,

---

23. What determines whether we are going to do the loving thing?
24, 25. How can you strengthen your motivation to show love?
26, 27. How does sharing things increase one's love?

Adam, lived in a paradise. All his physical needs were bountifully supplied. From the start he was surrounded by beauty. Not only were there meadows and flowers, woodlands and streams, but also there was an abundant variety of animal life subject to his domination as earth's caretaker. Yet with all of this, one need was not met: someone human with whom to share this paradise of beauty. Have you ever been alone as you gazed in amazement at a spectacular sunset, and wished that a loved one were there to share it with you? Or have you had exciting good news, but no one to tell it to? Jehovah God discerned Adam's need, and provided him a mate with whom to share his thoughts and feelings. Sharing brings two persons together, and helps love to take root and grow.

²⁷ Marriage is sharing. Perhaps there is an affectionate glance across the room, a touch, a soft word, even sitting peacefully together without speaking. Every act can manifest love: making a bed, washing the dishes, saving to buy something that she wants but won't ask for because of the budget, helping with the other's work when he or she is behind. Love means sharing the work and the play, the troubles and the joys, the accomplishments and the failures, the thoughts of the mind and the feelings of the heart. Share common goals, and reach them together. This is what makes two people one; this is what makes love grow.

²⁸ Serving your mate can help your love for him to mature. A wife commonly serves by cooking meals, making beds, cleaning house, washing clothes, caring for household business. The hus-

---

28. How does serving promote love?

band usually serves by providing the food she cooks, the beds she makes, the house she cleans, the clothes she washes. It is this serving, this giving, that brings happiness and nourishes love. As Jesus said, there is more happiness in giving than there is in receiving. Or, there is more happiness in serving than in being served. (Acts 20:35) He told his disciples that "the greatest among you must be your servant." (Matthew 23: 11, *New English Bible*) That view will eliminate any spirit of competitiveness and contribute to happiness. When we serve we feel needed, we are filling a purpose, and this gives us self-respect and makes us content. Marriage gives both husband and wife ample opportunity to serve and to find such contentment, thus cementing their marriage more strongly in love.

[29] What if one of the marriage mates is a Christian servant of God who practices these Biblical principles, but the other is not? Does this change the way a Christian should act? Not basically. There may not be as much talk about God's purposes on the part of the Christian, but the conduct is the same. The unbelieving mate has the same basic needs as a worshiper of Jehovah, and in some respects reacts in the same way. This is stated at Romans 2:14, 15: "Whenever people of the nations that do not have law do by nature the things of the law, these people, although not having law, are a law to themselves. They are the very ones who demonstrate the matter of the law to be written in their hearts, while their conscience is bearing witness with them and, between their own thoughts, they are being accused or even

29. Why will love appeal even to those who are not servants of God?

excused." Exemplary Christian conduct will usually be appreciated and will make love grow.

[30] Love does not wait for dramatic circumstances to reveal itself. In some respects, love is like clothing. What holds your clothing together? A few big knots tied with rope? Or thousands of little stitches of thread? The thousands of little stitches, and that is true whether we speak of literal clothing or spiritual "garments." It is the continuing accumulation of small words and acts manifested daily that "clothe" us and reveal what we are. Such spiritual "clothing" will not wear out and become valueless as does physical clothing. It is, as the Bible says, "incorruptible apparel." —1 Peter 3:4.

[31] Do you want your marriage to be held together by "a perfect bond of union"? Then do as recommended at Colossians 3:9, 10, 12, 14: "Strip off the old personality with its practices, and clothe yourselves with the new personality . . . clothe yourselves with the tender affections of compassion, kindness, lowliness of mind, mildness, and long-suffering . . . clothe yourselves with love, for it is a perfect bond of union."

---

30. Is love to be displayed only under dramatic circumstances? Why do you so answer?
31. What fine counsel on love is provided at Colossians 3:9, 10, 12, 14?

7

Having Children —A Responsibility and a Reward

G IVING BIRTH to children is a prospect that is both thrilling and sobering. It is an everyday occurrence among humankind, true. Yet each birth is the result of amazingly intricate processes. When we understand something about these we can better appreciate why the inspired psalmist was moved to say: "Look! Sons are an inheritance from Jehovah; the fruitage of the belly is a reward." (Psalm 127:3) Consider what happens.

² A sperm cell from a man unites with an egg cell in a woman. The two cells become one, and the one starts to divide. It becomes two, the two become four, the four become eight, until eventually this one cell has become, in a grown person, an estimated 60,000,000,000,000 cells! At first the new cells were all the same, then they began changing into different kinds—bone cells, muscle cells, nerve cells, liver cells, eye cells, skin cells, and so on and on.

³ Some of the mysteries of reproduction and differentiation have been uncovered, but many

1-4. (a) What are some of the amazing features about the development of a baby in the womb? (b) How does a knowledge of these things help you to appreciate Psalm 127:3?

remain. What makes the original cell start to divide? As the dividing continues, what makes the cells start changing into many different kinds? What makes these different kinds group together in special shapes, sizes and functions, to become a liver, a nose, a little toe? These changes start taking place at preset times. What controls the timetables? Also, this growing embryo in the mother's womb is a body with a genetic makeup different from hers. Normally her body rejects foreign tissues, such as skin grafts or organ transplants from other persons. Why doesn't it reject this genetically foreign embryo, instead of nourishing it for some 280 days?

⁴ All these amazing activities take place on schedule because Jehovah God programmed them into the one cell formed by the sperm and the egg. The psalmist indicates this when saying to the Creator: "Your eyes saw even the embryo of me, and in your book all its parts were down in writing, as regards the days when they were formed and there was not yet one among them." —Psalm 139:16.

DEVELOPMENT AND BIRTH

⁵ The embryo develops rapidly. By the fourth week it has a brain, a nervous system, and a circulatory system with a heart pumping blood through already placed vessels. Blood is manufactured by the yolk sac for six weeks; then the liver takes over this function, which is finally assumed by the bone marrow. In the fifth week arms and legs begin to form; in three more weeks fingers and toes appear. By the seventh week

5-8. Between the fourth week of pregnancy and the birth of a baby, what are some of the things that happen in the womb?

major muscle groups, along with eyes, ears, nose and mouth, have formed.

[6] "My bones," the psalmist continues, speaking to Jehovah God, "were not hidden from you when I was made in secret." (Psalm 139:15) In the ninth week cartilage is turning into bone as the skeleton is formed, and the developing baby is now called a fetus instead of an embryo. "You yourself produced my kidneys." (Psalm 139:13) The divine processes governing this occur in the fourth month and the kidneys now filter the blood.

[7] By this time the developing baby moves and twists about, curls its fingers or its toes when the palm of its hand or the sole of its foot feels a tickling sensation. It grips things with finger and thumb, and sucks its thumb and thereby exercises muscles later to be used for feeding at its mother's breasts. It hiccups, and the mother feels it jump. By the sixth month many organs are virtually complete. The nostrils have opened, eyebrows have appeared, soon the eyes will open, and ears will function so that even in the womb the infant can be startled by loud noises.

[8] At 40 weeks, labor starts. The mother's uterine muscles contract and the baby is on its way out into the world. In the process its head is often pressed out of shape, but, since its skull bones have not yet fused together, after delivery the head resumes its normal shape. Up until now the mother has done everything for the baby: provided oxygen, food, protection, warmth and also for the removal of wastes. Now the baby must go to work for itself, quickly, or it will die.

[9] It must start breathing in order for the lungs

9. For a baby to live outside the womb, what changes must take place quickly?

to put oxygen into the blood. But to do this another drastic conversion must take place instantaneously: the pathway of the circulating blood must change! While the fetus was in the womb, there was a hole in the wall of its heart. That wall separated the right and left chambers and kept much of the baby's blood from ever going toward the lungs. Of the blood that did, a large vessel made most of it bypass the lungs. In the womb, only about 10 percent of the blood went through the lungs; after birth all of it must do so, and immediately! To accomplish this, within seconds after birth the big vessel that bypassed the lungs constricts and the blood that went through it now goes to the lungs. Meanwhile the hole in the wall of the heart closes, and all the blood pumped from the right side of the heart now goes to the lungs to be oxygenated. The baby breathes, the blood is oxygenated, dramatic changes have been made and the baby lives! As the inspired psalmist so beautifully sums it up: "You kept me screened off in the belly of my mother. I shall laud you because in a fear-inspiring way I am wonderfully made."—Psalm 139:13, 14.

[10] With what gratitude married couples should view this gift from Jehovah! The power to produce a human creature, a child who is a part of both but different from either! Truly, "an inheritance from Jehovah"!

CARING FOR THE "INHERITANCE"

[11] It was more than morality that caused Jehovah God to establish the law that sex relations

---

10. Considering the amazing development of a baby in the womb, how should parents feel about their children?
11. What questions should those who are thinking about starting a family ask themselves, and why?

were to be limited to married couples. He also had in mind the arrival of children. A child needs both a father and a mother who love each other and who will love and cherish their offspring. The newborn child needs the warmth and security of a home, with a father and mother who want him and who will provide the environment needed for his growth and personality development. A husband and wife who are considering having a baby should ask themselves: Do we want a baby? Can we provide for its needs—not just physically, but emotionally and spiritually? Will we train it properly, set the right examples for it to follow? Are we willing to accept the responsibilities parenthood brings, accept the sacrifices involved? As children it may have seemed to us that our parents tied us down, but when we become parents we find what a time-consuming project rearing children really is. Yet with the responsibility of parenthood can come great joys.

¹² The decision has been made—whether by parents or by biological circumstances. You, the wife, are pregnant. Your care for this "inheritance from Jehovah" starts. Some things you must eat, and others you must avoid or limit. Foods rich in iron* are important, for in the womb the baby is storing up enough iron to last it for six months after its birth. You need more milk (cheese is also good) to supply the calcium your baby needs for building bones. And a balanced carbohydrate intake† will help to avoid excessive weight in-

---

* Such as meats, green and yellow vegetables.
† Involving starchy foods and those with considerable sugar content.

12-14. Once a woman is pregnant, how can she contribute toward the development of a healthy baby by (a) her diet? (b) what she does about alcohol, tobacco, drugs? (c) controlling her emotions?

crease. True, you may be eating for two of you, but one of you is very, very tiny!

[13] Other factors may or may not need to be considered, depending on the way you live. Alcoholic drinks send alcohol to the fetus, so caution is needed, as an excess could produce mental and physical retardation. Some babies have been born drunk because their mothers were heavy drinkers. Smoking puts nicotine into the bloodstream of the fetus, and also causes carbon monoxide to replace oxygen in its blood. Thus, the infant's prospects for normal health may be irreparably damaged even before it is born. Spontaneous abortion and stillborn babies are much more frequent among women who smoke. Addictive drugs taken by the mother can cause the baby to be born an addict, and some nonaddictive drugs taken medicinally may also prove dangerous, possibly crippling the baby. Even the excessive drinking of coffee is suspected of causing some damage.

[14] Additionally, emotional stress in the mother can change her hormone output and make the fetus overly active, thereby causing the newborn child to be restless and irritable. The growing baby may be 'screened off in the belly of its mother,' but it would be a mistake to think that it is totally cut off from the world around it. Through the mother it can be affected; she is its only connecting link with the outside world, and that puts her primarily "in the driver's seat" as to whether the effect is good or bad. The way she cares for herself and how she reacts to circumstances will make the difference. It goes without saying that in this she needs the cooperation of those around her, and especially the love and care of her husband.—Compare 1 Samuel 4:19.

DECISIONS YOU MUST MAKE

[15] Will you have your baby in a hospital or at home? In some cases there may be little choice. In many areas hospitals may not even be available. In other areas having a baby at home may be a rarity and may present risks due to lack of experienced help, such as that of a midwife. Wherever possible, it is always good to be examined during pregnancy by a doctor, to know whether you can expect a normal delivery or one accompanied by complications.

[16] Will you have your baby under anesthesia or by natural childbirth? You and your husband must decide, after weighing advantages and disadvantages. Natural childbirth may involve the husband in the momentous event. The baby is immediately put with its mother. Some believe that these are advantages to be seriously considered, if examinations indicate that the birth will be without complications. Some researchers contend that babies born under the more peaceful conditions of natural childbirth have fewer emotional problems and psychosomatic illnesses.

[17] The magazine *Psychology Today,* December 1977 issue, states:

> "Psychologists have known for decades that the first year of a baby's life can have an enduring impact on his later mental and physical development. It now appears that the baby's first day —perhaps even his first 60 minutes—is just as crucial. The emotional bond that the mother forms toward the child, and the kind of care she begins to give him, are particularly important after de-

15, 16. What decisions may need to be made about the place and manner of childbirth?
17-19. What has research revealed about the advisability of a baby's being with the mother as soon as possible after birth?

livery. Recent studies also demonstrate that the first hours may have a lot to do with shaping the mother's attitude toward the child, the strength of her commitment to him, and her capacity for mothering."

[18] If the mother does not have general anesthesia during the birth, the baby will be alert, have its eyes open, look around, follow movements, turn toward human voices, and be especially aware of the higher-pitched female voice. Eye contact between mother and child can be quickly established. This seems to be important, and in some studies mothers reported that once their baby looked at them they felt much closer to it. Body contact, skin to skin, of mother and baby right after birth is considered advantageous to both.

[19] Researchers claim that the problems of babies treated by medical centers can sometimes be traced to the first few hours of life. Comparisons made between children given the standard hospital treatment at birth and others immediately put with their mothers indicate that after one month the babies delivered by natural childbirth were doing better. "Even more striking," *Psychology Today* states, "at five years of age, the children of extended-contact mothers had significantly higher IQ's [evidence of intelligence] and more advanced scores on language tests than children who were treated according to standard hospital procedure."

[20] In all of this, however, circumstances must be seriously weighed. We should not lose from view the fact that our first human parents left us a legacy of imperfection. This inevitably robs "nat-

20. To make a wise decision on these matters, what else must be kept in mind?

ural birth" today of some of its naturalness, and our inherited defects can cause complications. (Genesis 3:16; 35:16-19; 38:27-29) Let your decisions be governed by your personal circumstances and what you believe to be wisest in your case, whether this matches the "ideal" birth others may aim at or does not.

21 Will you breast-feed your baby? There are many advantages to both you and your baby. Mother's milk is the perfect food for infants. It is easy to digest, and it protects against infection, intestinal disorders and respiratory problems. For the first few days the breasts secrete colostrum, a yellowish fluid especially good for infants because (1) it is low in fats and carbohydrates and hence easier to digest, (2) it is richer in immunity factors than the mother's milk that will come in a few days, and (3) it has a slightly laxative effect that helps clear out the cells, mucus and bile that collected in the infant's bowels before birth.

22 Breast-feeding benefits the mother. It reduces bleeding in the mother because the baby's sucking stimulates the uterus to contract. The sucking also stimulates the breasts to produce more milk, and mothers who feared they could not produce enough milk discover that there is no shortage. Regular breast-feeding *in some cases* postpones the resumption of ovulation and the menstrual cycle, and to that extent tends to be a natural contraceptive. The American Cancer Society says that "mothers who breast feed show less cases of cancer of the breast." Breast-feeding also benefits the family budget!

21, 22. What are some benefits of breast-feeding?

CHILD DEVELOPMENT
—HOW WILL YOU AIM THE ARROW?

[23] "Like arrows in the hand of a warrior, so are the children of one's youth. How happy is the man whose quiver is filled with them!" (Psalm 127:4, 5, *An American Translation*) The value of an arrow is determined by how well it is aimed as it leaves the bow. An arrow must be aimed with care and skill so that it will hit the target. In like manner, it is vital that, as parents, you wisely and prayerfully ponder on the kind of start in life you will give to your child. Will he or she on leaving your care become a balanced and mature adult, respected by others and an honor to God?

[24] Decisions should be made before the baby's arrival as to its care and training. The parents basically are the firstborn baby's whole world. What will that world be like? Will it show that the parents have taken to heart this counsel from God's Word: "Let all malicious bitterness and anger and wrath and screaming and abusive speech be taken away from you along with all badness. But become kind to one another, tenderly compassionate, freely forgiving one another just as God also by Christ freely forgave you"? (Ephesians 4:31, 32) Whatever the homelife is, it will be reflected in the infant child. Strive to make your baby's world one of peace and security, of warmth and love. The baby that is cherished will absorb these qualities and they will shape its emotions accordingly. Your feelings will be sensed, your examples followed. The genetic laws of our Creator made marvelous provisions for the baby's

---

23. What principles about child training are implied at Psalm 127:4, 5?
24. (a) What kind of home environment should parents strive to make for their children? (b) Why is this important?

development in the womb; how will you shape it outside the womb? So much depends on the home conditions you provide. This, as much as the genes, determines what kind of adult the baby will become. "Train up a boy according to the way for him; even when he grows old he will not turn aside from it."—Proverbs 22:6.

[25] Neither man nor woman can produce a single blade of grass, but together they can produce another human, one of infinite complexity and different from any other person on the earth! An amazing accomplishment, so amazing that it is hard to believe that so many today fail to appreciate the sacredness of the responsibility that goes with it! People will plant flowers, water them, fertilize them, keep them free of weeds—all to get a beautiful garden. Should we not take far more time and exert more effort to make children become beautiful?

[26] A married couple have a right to have children. Their children have a corresponding right to have parents, not just in name but in fact. A Christian dedicated to God may spend much time and energy in sharing Bible knowledge in the hope of making one disciple, and yet not always succeed. Should not Christian parents spend even more time to 'bring up their own children in the discipline and mental-regulating of Jehovah'? (Ephesians 6:4) If they rear one child to be a fine servant of the Giver of life, Jehovah God, is that not cause for great rejoicing? Then, indeed, their having given birth to that son or daughter will prove to be richly rewarded.—Proverbs 23:24, 25.

___

25, 26. Why is it reasonable for parents to give much time and attention to their children?

[27] Psalm 128:3 likens children to olive plants: "Your wife will be like a fruit-bearing vine in the innermost parts of your house. Your sons will be like slips of olive trees all around your table." Trees may be shaped in different ways by training them. Some are made to grow flat against a wall. Others spread out low over the ground. Some are even made small and stunted by trimming their roots and cramping them, as in the case of a bonsai. An old saying emphasizes how early training will also shape a child: "The way the twig is bent is the way the tree will grow." A sense of balance is needed here. On the one hand, the child needs guiding so that it will conform to righteous standards. At the same time it should not be expected to conform to some preconceived ideal the parents have as to the exact personality it should display. You cannot make an olive tree bear figs. Train your child in right ways but do not force it into a predetermined mold that will not allow its distinctive personality and inherited gifts to find normal expression. Give yourself time to come to know this child you have produced. Then, as with a tender young tree, give your child guidance that is strong enough to protect and support it in a right direction, yet gentle enough not to cramp the child's development to its full capacity for good.

A REWARD FROM JEHOVAH

[28] Jacob of ancient times showed his concern for the care of his children. When a journey was pro-

---

27. In guiding the development of a child, why should the child's own personality be considered?
28. How can we benefit from what Genesis 33:5, 13, 14 says about Jacob's concern for his children?

Closeness now avoids
generation gap later

posed, the pace of which might have been too much for them, Jacob said to the one making the proposal: "My lord is aware that the children are delicate and sheep and cattle that are giving suck are in my charge, and should they drive them too quickly for one day, then the whole flock will certainly die. Let my lord, please, pass on ahead of his servant, but may I myself continue the journey at my leisure according to the pace of the livestock that is before me and according to the pace of the children." When meeting his brother, Esau, earlier he was asked, "Who are these with you?" Jacob's response was, "The children with whom God has favored your servant." (Genesis 33:5, 13, 14) Parents today should not only show merciful consideration to their children as Jacob did, but also view them as he did—as a favor from Jehovah. Of course, before getting married, a man should weigh seriously whether he can support a wife and children. The Bible counsels: "First put all in order out of doors and make everything ready on the land; then establish your house and home." (Proverbs 24:27, *New English Bible*) In harmony with this practical advice, a man should make preparations for marriage and family life beforehand. Then, even an unplanned pregnancy will be greeted with joy and not dreaded as a financial burden.

²⁹ The matter of having children clearly merits being considered very seriously, not only as regards the firstborn but also for any thereafter. Are parents finding it difficult to feed, care for and train the children they already have? Then

---

29. Why should the matter of having children be given serious advance consideration?

respect for their Creator as well as the quality of love should certainly move them to ponder what self-control they can exercise to slow down further increase in the family.

³⁰ Really, whose child is it? Yours, in one sense. But, in another sense, the child belongs to the Creator. You are entrusted with its care, just as your parents were entrusted with your care as a child. But you were not actually your parents' property to be treated in just any way they might please; nor is your child your property in that sense. Parents cannot direct or control the moment of conception nor the development of the child in the womb. They cannot even see or fully understand the marvelous processes involved. (Psalm 139:13, 15; Ecclesiastes 11:5) If some physical imperfection causes a miscarriage or a stillbirth, they cannot bring the dead child to life. Thus, we need to recognize humbly that God is the Life-Giver of us all, and we all belong to him: "To Jehovah belong the earth and that which fills it, the productive land and those dwelling in it."—Psalm 24:1.

³¹ You are responsible for the children you bring into the world and also accountable to the Creator as to how you rear them. He created the earth, purposed that it be inhabited, and equipped our first human parents with procreative power to accomplish that purpose. Their defection from him placed them on the side of the Adversary who challenged God's rightful exercise of his sovereignty over his family of creatures in heaven

---

30. (a) Why can we say that a child really belongs to God? (b) How should this affect the viewpoint of parents?
31, 32. (a) What responsibility before God do parents have? (b) What results from caring properly for that responsibility?

and on earth. By training your children to grow up as persons of integrity to their Creator, you and your family can prove that Adversary false and Jehovah God true. As Proverbs 27:11 states: "Be wise, my son, and make my heart rejoice, that I may make a reply to him that is taunting me."

[32] Fulfilling your obligation to your children, together with your responsibility to God, can bring you a sense of true accomplishment in life. You will be able to join in wholehearted appreciation of the saying of Psalm 127:3: "The fruitage of the belly is a reward."

8

Your Role as Parents

IN LIFE many events affect us to a very limited degree. Others have a major and lasting effect. The birth of a child is clearly one of the latter. For a husband and wife, life will never be the same thereafter. Though very small, the new personality in the home will make itself felt with a voice and a presence that cannot be ignored.

² Life for the parents should be richer and happier. But it does present a challenge, and, for the finest results, that challenge needs to be met by both parents. It took both of you to produce the child, and both of you will play a vital role in your baby's development from birth onward. The need for sincere, united—and humble—co-operation was never greater.

³ Understanding the role of each parent and how these roles can harmonize should help greatly in meeting the needs of your baby, producing happy results. Balance is needed. Even though the mind strives to be reasonable, emotions often push things off balance. We may tend to go to extremes, from too little to too much, and back again to too little. It is desirable for the father to exercise his headship, but, if he overdoes it, he becomes overbearing. It is good for the mother

---

1-3. (a) What effect can the birth of a baby have on parents? (b) Why is it important for both father and mother to understand their roles as parents?

to share in training and disciplining the children, but to take over these duties to the exclusion of the father undermines the family structure. Good is good, but a good thing may become bad if carried to an extreme.—Philippians 4:5.

THE MOTHER'S CRUCIAL ROLE

[4] A newborn baby is totally dependent on its mother for its immediate needs. If she lovingly supplies these needs the baby feels secure. (Psalm 22:9, 10) It must be well fed and kept clean and warm; but supplying physical needs is not enough. Emotional needs are just as important. If the baby does not receive love, it becomes insecure. A mother can soon learn to tell how great the need really is when her infant calls for attention. But if its cries are consistently ignored it may become ill. If it is emotionally deprived over a period of time it may be stunted emotionally for the rest of its life.

[5] Experiments in many different places have confirmed this fact: Babies become sick and even die if deprived of love, as expressed through talking and touching, stroking and cuddling. (Compare Isaiah 66:12; 1 Thessalonians 2:7.) Though others may do this, the mother, in whose womb the baby came to life and was nurtured for the first months of life, is beyond all question the one most logically suited to do this. There is a natural interaction that takes place between mother and child. Her instinctive desire to hold the newborn baby close to her is matched by the infant's instinctive searching for her breast.

4. What are some things that a baby needs from its mother?
5-7. According to recent research, how is a baby affected by its mother's love and attention?

⁶ Research has shown that the brain of an infant is very active and that mental development is promoted when its senses of feeling, hearing, seeing and smelling are stimulated. When an infant nurses, it perceives the warmth and smell of the mother's skin. It looks almost continuously at her face as she feeds it. It hears not only her voice as she talks or sings to it but also her heartbeat, a sound that it heard while yet in the womb. In a Norwegian publication, child psychologist Anne-Marit Duve observes:

> "Since the activity of the pupils clearly shows the degree of brain activity, we have reason to believe that a high degree of skin stimulation, a high degree of contact—not the least the contact connected with nursing—can stimulate the mental activity, which in turn can lead to greater intellectual capacity in adulthood."

⁷ So, when the baby frequently feels the mother's touch, as she picks it up, cuddles it or bathes and dries it, the stimulation it receives plays an important part in its development and what it will be like in later life. While getting up at night and spending time in soothing a crying infant may not be the most enjoyable pastime, the knowledge of the later benefits can compensate considerably for the loss of sleep.

LEARNING LOVE BY BEING LOVED

⁸ The baby's being loved is vitally important for its emotional development. It learns to love by being loved, by exposure to examples of love. Speaking of love for God, 1 John 4:19 says, "We love, because he first loved us." The initial lessons

8-10. (a) What does a baby learn from its mother's love? (b) Why is this important?

The mother's look and touch and tone of voice tell her baby, "I love you"

in love fall mainly to the mother. A mother bends over a baby in its bed, puts her hand on its chest and jiggles it gently as she puts her face close to the baby's and says, 'I see you! I see you!' The baby, of course, doesn't know the words (which really aren't particularly logical anyway). But it wriggles and coos with delight, for it recognizes that the playful hand and the tone of voice are clearly saying to it, 'I love you! I love you!' It is reassured and feels secure.

[9] Babies and small children who are shown love appreciate it, and, in imitation of that love, they practice it, putting small arms around the mother's neck and giving enthusiastic kisses. They are pleased with the heartwarming emotional response they reap from their mother as a result. They begin to learn the vital lesson that there is happiness in giving love as well as in receiving it, that by sowing love they reap it in return. (Acts 20:35; Luke 6:38) Evidence shows that if an early attachment to the mother is not made, later on the child may find it very difficult to make deep attachments and commitments to others.

[10] Since children start learning immediately after birth, the first few years are the most vital ones. During those years the mother's love is crucial. If she succeeds in showing and teaching love—not indulgence—she can do lasting good; if she fails she can do lasting harm. Being a good mother is one of the most challenging and rewarding jobs a woman can have. Despite all its strains and demands, what "career" occupation that the world offers can begin to approach it in significance and lasting satisfaction?

THE VITAL ROLE OF THE FATHER

¹¹ It is natural that in early infancy the mother plays a more prominent role in the child's life. But from the baby's birth onward the father should also be a part of the baby's world. Even when the child is still an infant, the father can and should get involved, caring for the baby at times, playing with it, comforting it when it cries. In this way the father gets established in the child's mind. The father's role should gradually come to take on greater prominence as time passes. If he waits too long to begin, it can be the start of a problem that surfaces especially when the child becomes a teen-ager and discipline becomes more difficult. The teen-age son especially may need his father's help. But if a good relationship has not been established before, the gulf produced over a period of years cannot be bridged in a few weeks.

¹² Whether the child is a boy or a girl, the influence of the father's masculine qualities can make a vital contribution to the development of a rounded-out, balanced personality. God's Word shows that the father is to be the head of the family. He is responsible to provide materially for them. (1 Corinthians 11:3; 1 Timothy 5:8) Yet, "not by bread alone does man live but by every expression of Jehovah's mouth does man live." As regards his children, the father is also commanded to "go on bringing them up in the discipline and mental-regulating of Jehovah." (Deuteronomy 8:3; Ephesians 6:4) While natural

---

11. (a) How can the father establish his role in the child's mind? (b) Why is this vital?
12, 13. (a) What is the father's role in the family? (b) How can a father's fulfilling his responsibilities in the right way affect his children's view of authority?

affection for his offspring should motivate him, it is, above all, a sense of responsibility to his Creator that should move him to do his best to fulfill the divine commission that is his.

¹³ Along with the warmth, tenderness and compassion that a mother expresses, the father can contribute a stabilizing influence, one of strength and of wise direction. The way he handles his God-given assignment can have a marked effect on his children's later attitude toward authority, both human and divine, as to whether they respect it and how well they can work under another's direction without chafing or rebelling.

¹⁴ If he has a son, the father's example and handling of matters can do much to determine whether the boy grows up to be a weak, indecisive person, or one who is manly, steady, showing courage of conviction and a willingness to shoulder responsibility. It can affect the kind of husband or father the son eventually becomes—a rigid, unreasoning, harsh one, or one who is balanced, discerning and kind. If there is a daughter in the family, her father's influence and relationship can affect her whole outlook on the male sex and either contribute to or hinder her future success in marriage. The effect of this paternal influence begins from infancy.

¹⁵ The extensiveness of the father's responsibility to teach is shown in God's instructions to his people at Deuteronomy 6:6, 7: "These words that I am commanding you today must prove to be on your heart; and you must inculcate them in your son and speak of them when you sit in your

---

14. What effect can the father's good example have on his son or daughter?
15, 16. (a) What responsibility of teaching does the Bible place on a father? (b) How can this be discharged?

Do you plan activities with your children?

house and when you walk on the road and when you lie down and when you get up."

¹⁶ Not just the words themselves that are found in God's Word but also the *message* they convey must be impressed daily on the child's mind. Opportunities are always there. Flowers in a garden, insects in the air, birds or squirrels in the trees, seashells on the beach, pinecones in the mountains, stars twinkling in the night sky—all these wonders speak of the Creator, and you should interpret to your children the meaning of their utterances. The psalmist says: "The heavens are declaring the glory of God; and of the work of his hands the expanse is telling. One day after another day causes speech to bubble forth, and one night after another night shows forth knowledge." (Psalm 19:1, 2) By being alert to use these things, and especially to draw upon the daily affairs of life in illustrating and emphasizing right principles and in showing the wisdom and benefit of God's counsel, the father can build up in the mind and heart of his child the most essential basis for the future: the conviction not only that God is, but that 'he rewards those who earnestly seek him.' —Hebrews 11:6.

¹⁷ Discipline is also part of the father's role. "What son is he that a father does not discipline?" is the question asked at Hebrews 12:7. But it is his obligation to do this in a way that does not go to extremes, overcorrecting to the point of irritation or even harassment. To fathers, God's Word says, "Do not be exasperating your children, so that they do not become downhearted." (Colossians 3:21) Restrictions are necessary, but some-

---

17, 18. (a) How should a father discipline his children? (b) What is more effective than the making of many rules?

times we can multiply and expand rules until they become burdensome and discouraging.

[18] The Pharisees of ancient times were lovers of rules; they accumulated heaps of them and produced crops of hypocrites. It is a human failing to think that problems can be solved simply by making additional rules; but life's experiences make plain that reaching the heart is the real key. So be sparing on rules; try instead to instill principles, aiming in the direction that God himself does: "I will put my laws in their mind, and in their hearts I shall write them."—Hebrews 8:10.

FATHER AND MOTHER ARE PARTNERS

[19] The father usually makes the living, and when he comes home from work he may be tired, and he still may have other duties to perform. But he should make time for his wife and for his children. He must communicate with his family, set aside time for family discussions and family projects, for family fun or outings. In this way family unity and solidarity are built up. Perhaps before the children came he and his wife spent much time outside the home. But for them to keep on in that way, running here and there and possibly keeping late hours, would not be living up to the responsibility of parenthood. It would be very unfair to their offspring. Sooner or later, the parents would pay the price for their lack of regularity and of responsibility. Like adults, children fare better when their life has a basic stability and regularity; this contributes to mental, physical and emotional health. The daily routine of family life will have its full comple-

---

19. What might be done to ensure good communication in the home?

ment of ups and downs without parents needlessly adding to these.—Compare Matthew 6:34; Colossians 4:5.

[20] The father and the mother should cooperate in dealing with the children, teaching them, setting limits for them, disciplining them, loving them. 'A house divided against itself cannot stand.' (Mark 3:25) Parents do well to discuss the discipline to be followed; they can then avoid having their children witness any disunity regarding discipline. To do otherwise could invite the children to try to 'divide and conquer.' True, it may happen that on some occasion a parent will react hastily or in anger and administer discipline that is extreme, or, when all the facts are considered, perhaps was really not called for at all. It may be possible for the parents to talk about it privately and then the parent who acted unwisely may choose personally to rectify matters with the child. Or, where this private talk is not possible, the parent who feels that to support the mate would mean supporting an injustice may say something like, 'I understand why you feel angry, and I would feel the same way. But there may be something you weren't aware of, and that is . . .' thereafter clarifying whatever may have been overlooked. This can have a calming influence without showing division or disagreement in the presence of the disciplined child. As the inspired proverb says: "By presumptuousness one only causes a struggle, but with those consulting together there is wisdom."—Proverbs 13:10; see also Ecclesiastes 7:8.

---

20. When it comes to disciplining children, what can parents do so that they will be united in their efforts?

²¹ The Hebrew Scriptures show disciplining to be a dual role: "Listen, my son, to the discipline of your father, and do not forsake the law of your mother." The Christian Greek Scriptures do likewise: "Children, be obedient to your *parents* in union with the Lord, for this is righteous." Sometimes the father views disciplining the children as his wife's job. Or, a wife may take the opposite view and do no more than threaten a misbehaving child with 'Just wait till your father gets home!' But if there is to be family happiness, and each parent is to receive the children's love and respect, the duty needs to be shared.—Proverbs 1:8; Ephesians 6:1.

²² Children need to see their parents' united cooperation in this and the willingness of each to shoulder his or her responsibility. If a begging child always hears his father say, 'Go ask your mother,' or the mother invariably passes the decision back to the father, then the parent who finds that the request requires him (or her) to answer "No" is cast in the role of villain. Of course, there may be circumstances where the father may say, 'Yes, you can go outside for a while—but check first with your mother to see when supper will be ready.' Or the mother at times may feel that, while some request does not seem objectionable to her, her husband should express himself on the matter. But both will be alert to see that in no way do they encourage or allow the child to pit one parent against the other to gain his objective. The wise wife will also

21. Should discipline be left up to only one parent? Why or why not?
22. What should be avoided when handling a child's requests, and why?

guard against using her share of authority in a competitive way, trying through indulgence to gain the major share of the child's affection at her husband's expense.

[23] Actually, in family decisions each member may have areas where his decision merits special consideration. The father has the responsibility of deciding on questions involving the overall welfare of the family, often deciding these after discussion with the others and giving consideration to their wishes and preferences. The mother may make the decisions regarding the kitchen and many other household matters. (Proverbs 31:11, 27) As they grow up, children might be allowed to make certain decisions about their play areas, some choice of clothing, or some other personal things. But there should be enough parental oversight to see that sound principles are followed, the children's safety is not endangered and the rights of others are not infringed upon. This can give children a gradual start in decision-making.

IS HONORING YOU PARENTS EASY?

[24] Children are told, "Honor your father and your mother." (Ephesians 6:2; Exodus 20:12) For them to do this is also honoring God's commandment. Do you make it easy for them? Wife, you are told to honor and respect your husband. Isn't it very hard for you to do so if he makes little or no effort to live up to what God's Word requires of him? Husband, you are to cherish and honor your wife as your loved helpmate. Isn't it

---

23. In a family, is decision-making necessarily limited to the father?
24. The fact that children are to honor their father and their mother places what responsibility on parents?

difficult, if she is not helpful? Make it easy then for your children to obey God's command that they honor you, their parents. Earn their respect by providing a peaceful home, a good set of standards, good examples in your own conduct, sound teaching and training, and loving discipline when needed.

[25] "Two are better than one," observed King Solomon, "because they have a good reward for their hard work." (Ecclesiastes 4:9) When two people walk together and one falls, the other is there to help him up. So, too, in the family the husband and wife can support and encourage each other in their respective roles. In so many areas of parenthood those roles overlap, and this is good for the unity of the family. Children should bring the parents closer together, uniting them in a common training work. But sometimes divisive questions may arise over how the child is to be trained and disciplined. Sometimes a wife showers so much attention on the child that her husband feels neglected, even resentful. This can affect his attitude toward the child. He may be cool toward it, or he may, instead, shower affection on it but lessen his attention to his wife. A high price is paid when the husband or the wife gets off balance.

[26] Yet another problem may arise when a new baby arrives and there is already an older child. The mother must spend a great deal of time with the new baby. To keep the older child from feeling neglected and jealous, the father might give extra attention to the older child.

---

25. What problems can arise when parents are not united as to how the children should be trained?
26. What might be done to keep an older child from feeling jealous when the mother must devote much of her time to a new baby?

²⁷ Certainly two are better than one, but one is better than none. It may be that the mother is the one who, by circumstance, must bring up the children without a father's help. Or, the father may face this same challenge. Many times homes are religiously divided, in that one parent, as a servant of Jehovah God, has full faith in the counsel of the Bible, and the other parent does not. Where the dedicated Christian is the husband, he, as the family head, has more control of the course to be followed in the training and disciplining of the children. Nevertheless, he may need to show great patience, self-control and endurance; he should be firm where a serious issue exists, yet reasonable and kind even though under provocation, and be flexible wherever circumstances will allow. If the believer is the wife, and hence subject to the husband, the way she proceeds will depend greatly on his attitude. Is he merely not interested in the Bible, or does he oppose his wife's practice of her beliefs and her endeavors to teach them to the children? If he opposes her, she must depend on the course the apostle outlined: By the wife's exemplary care of her duties and her respectful attitude, her husband "may be won without a word." She will also use what opportunities are available to her to train her children in Bible principles.—1 Peter 3:1-4.

THE HOME ENVIRONMENT

²⁸ The role of both parents is to provide a home atmosphere of love. If this is felt by the children, their uncertainties or mistakes will not pile up in-

---

27. When one of the marriage mates is an unbeliever, how can children be helped spiritually?
28, 29. What kind of home environment is desirable, and why?

side of them because they are afraid to tell their parents. They know they can communicate and be understood, and that matters will be handled with loving concern. (Compare 1 John 4:17-19; Hebrews 4:15, 16.) Home will be not only a shelter but also a haven. Parental affection will make the children's spirits grow and flourish.

[29] You cannot put a sponge into vinegar and expect it to fill with water. It can absorb only what surrounds it. The sponge will absorb water only if it is submerged in it. Children, too, absorb their surroundings. They sense the attitudes and observe the things practiced around them, and these they absorb like sponges. Children sense your feelings, whether these are nervous tensions or relaxed peacefulness. Even babies absorb the qualities of the home atmosphere, so one of faith, love, spirituality and reliance on Jehovah God is invaluable.

[30] Ask yourself: What standards do you expect your child to meet? Do both of you parents measure up to them? What does your family stand for? What kind of examples for the child are you? Do you complain, find fault, criticize others, dwell on negative thoughts? Is that the kind of children you want? Or, do you have high standards for your family, live up to them, and expect your children to do likewise? Do they understand that to belong to this family certain requirements are to be met, certain conduct is acceptable, and certain actions and attitudes are not? Children want to feel the security of belonging, so let them feel your approval and acceptance when they meet

---

30. What questions might parents ask themselves to determine whether they are providing fine guidance for their children?

the family standards. People have a way of living up to what is expected of them. Rate your child bad and he'll probably prove you right. Expect good from him, and you encourage him to live up to that.

[31] People are judged by their actions more than by their words. Children, too, may not give as much attention to words as to actions and they are often alert to detect any hypocrisy. Too many words may confuse children. Make sure your words are backed up by your practice of them. —1 John 3:18.

[32] Whether you are a father or a mother, your role is a challenging one. But the challenge can be met with happy results by following the counsel of the Giver of life. Carry out your assigned role conscientiously, as unto Him. (Colossians 3:17) Avoid extremes, keep your balance and "let your reasonableness become known to all," including your children.—Philippians 4:5.

31. What should always back up parental direction?
32. Whose counsel should always be followed?

9

Training Children from Infancy

THE mind of a newborn child has been compared to a page on which nothing is written. Actually, many impressions were made on the infant's mind even while it was in its mother's womb. And certain personality traits are indelibly written into it through genetic inheritance. But an enormous capacity for learning is there from the moment of birth onward. Rather than a single page, it is as if a whole library were waiting to receive the imprints of information on its pages.

[2] A baby's brain at birth is only one fourth the weight it will be in adulthood. But the brain grows so rapidly that in just two years it reaches three fourths of its adult weight! Intellectual growth keeps pace. Researchers say that a child's intelligence grows as much during the first four years of life as during the next thirteen. In fact, some state that "the concepts the child learns before his fifth birthday are among the most difficult he'll ever encounter."

[3] Such basic concepts as right and left, up and down, full and empty, as well as comparative degrees of size and weight all seem so natural to us. But a child must learn these and a host of

---

1-4. What evidence is there that a young child has tremendous capacity for learning?

114

other concepts. The very concept of speech must be implanted and established in the baby's mind.

[4] Language is rated by some as "probably the most difficult intellectual accomplishment a human being is ever called upon to perform." If you have ever struggled to learn a new language you will likely agree. But you at least have the advantage of knowing how language works. A baby does not, and yet its mind is capable of grasping the concept of language and putting it to work. Not only that, but children of tender years living in bilingual homes or areas may even speak two languages with ease—before they have even begun to go to school! So, the intelligence is there, waiting to be developed.

THE TIME TO START IS RIGHT AWAY!

[5] Writing to his companion Timothy, the apostle Paul reminded him that he had known the holy writings "from infancy." (2 Timothy 3:15) It is a wise parent who recognizes an infant's natural hunger to learn. Babies are very observant, all eyes and ears. Whether parents are aware of it or not, little ones are busy taking in information, filing it away, adding to it, drawing conclusions. Actually, if parents are not cautious, in a short time the infant may learn remarkably well just how to manipulate them according to its wishes. So, the admonition given in God's Word applies from birth onward: "Train up a boy according to the way for him; even when he grows old he will not turn aside from it." (Proverbs 22:6) The first lessons, of course, are as to love, with lots of loving care and affection. But along with this must come necessary correction applied gently but firmly.

---

5. How soon should the training of a child begin?

⁶ Talk to the infant, not in "baby talk" but in simple grown-up speech, which is what you want it to learn. When the small child learns to talk he will deluge you with questions: 'Why does it rain? Where did I come from? Where do the stars go in daytime? What are you doing? Why this? Why that?' On they come, endlessly! Listen to them, for questions are among a child's best tools for learning. Stifling the questions can stifle mental development.

⁷ But remember, as did the apostle, that "when I was a babe, I used to speak as a babe, to think as a babe, to reason as a babe." (1 Corinthians 13:11) Answer the questions as best you can, but simply and briefly. When a child asks, 'Why does it rain?' it doesn't want a complicated, detailed answer. Some reply such as, 'The clouds get heavy with water and the water falls,' may satisfy. A child's attention span is short; it quickly moves on to other fields. So just as you give the child milk until it progresses to solid foods, give it simple information until it can understand more detailed knowledge.—Compare Hebrews 5:13, 14.

⁸ Learning should be progressive. As mentioned, Timothy was acquainted with the Scriptures from infancy. Evidently his very earliest recollections from childhood included being taught from the Bible. Surely this was progressive, much as a father or mother today would begin teaching a child to read. Read to your child. When he is an

---

6. (a) With what kind of speech is it best to talk to a child? (b) What view should be taken of the many questions that a child may raise?

7. How might a young child's questions best be answered, and why?

8, 9. What could be done to teach a child progressively how to read?

Make learning a pleasant experience

infant, take him in your lap, with your arm around him and read in a pleasant voice. He will have a warm feeling of security and joy, and the reading will be a pleasant experience, regardless of how little he comprehends. Later, you may teach him the alphabet, as a game perhaps. Then make words, and eventually form the words into sentences. And make the process of learning a joy, as far as possible.

⁹ One couple, for example, would read aloud with their three-year-old child, pointing out each word for the child to follow as they went along. At certain words they would pause, and the child would supply the word, such as "God," "Jesus," "man," "tree." Gradually the words he was able to read increased, and at four years of age he was reading most of the words. Along with reading comes writing, first individual letters, and then complete words. To write his own name thrills a child!

¹⁰ Each child is different, with a unique personality, and should be helped to develop in harmony with its individual inherited potential and gifts. If you train each child to develop its inherited strengths and abilities, it will not need to feel envy at the accomplishments of other children. Each child should be loved and appreciated for itself. While helping it to overcome or control wrong inclinations, you should not try to force the child into a predetermined mold. Rather, guide it to the best use of its own good personality traits.

¹¹ A parent can foster a spirit of selfish competition by implying either the superiority or

10. Why is it wise to aid each child to develop its own potential?
11. Why is it unwise to compare one child unfavorably with another?

the inferiority of one child as compared with another. Whereas little children early in life show signs of inborn selfishness, they are initially free from ideas of rank, superiority, and feelings of self-importance. That is why Jesus could use a little child as an example to correct the spirit of ambition and concern for personal importance his disciples showed on a certain occasion. (Matthew 18:1-4) So, avoid comparing one child unfavorably with another. The child may take this as a rejection. First it will feel hurt, and if this treatment continues, it will likely turn hostile. On the other hand, the child presented as superior may become haughty and incur the dislike of others. As a parent, your love and acceptance should never be dependent upon how one child compares with another. Variety is delightful. An orchestra has many different kinds of instruments to add variety and richness, yet all are in harmony. Different personalities add flavor and interest to the family circle, yet harmony will not be impaired when all pattern themselves after their Creator's right principles.

HELP YOUR CHILD TO GROW

[12] God's Word says that 'it does not belong to man that walks to direct his steps.' (Jeremiah 10:23) Men say it does. So they refuse divine direction, accept human direction, walk into one difficulty after another, and end up proving God true after all. Jehovah God says there is a way that seems right to a man, but its end is the way of death. (Proverbs 14:12) Men have long taken the way that seemed right to *them*, and it has led to war, famine, sickness and death. If the way

---

12. What facts about adults demonstrate that a child needs proper direction?

that seems right to a grown, experienced man ends in death, how can the way that seems right to a child end elsewhere? If it does not belong to man that walks to direct his steps, how can it belong to the child that toddles to direct his way of life? The Creator provides directions for both parent and child through His Word.

[13] To parents, God says: "These words that I am commanding you today must prove to be on your heart; and you must inculcate them in your son and speak of them when you sit in your house and when you walk on the road and when you lie down and when you get up." (Deuteronomy 6:6, 7) At any and all times, whenever suitable opportunities present themselves, instruction should be given. If the family breakfasts together, even though for many the morning may be a rush time with getting ready for work or school, an expression of thanks for food will direct thoughts toward the Creator and can include other points of spiritual value to the family. Time may allow for some comment about the day's coming activities or about school and sound counsel on coping with problems that may likely arise. Bedtime, "when you lie down," can be a happy time for little children if parents give them some extra attention then. Bedtime stories can mean a lot to little ones and can be a fine means of teaching. The Bible is filled with material that only needs some parental ingenuity and warmth to make it very enjoyable to the child. Personal experiences from your own life will have special appeal to your children and can bring home some fine lessons. And though it may seem a challenge to

13, 14. How might parents instruct children, in harmony with the admonition found at Deuteronomy 6:6, 7?

find new stories to relate, often you will find that
the child likes to hear the same ones over and over
again. You may find that, by taking this extra
time, the lines of communication with your children will be made far more open. Prayer with
little ones at bedtime can also help establish early
communication with the One who can do the most
to guide and protect them.—Ephesians 3:20;
Philippians 4:6, 7.

¹⁴ Wherever you are, 'sitting at home' or travel-
ing 'on the road,' there are opportunities for you
to train your child in ways that are interesting
and effective. For children, some of this can be
in the form of a game. One couple gave this account of how this worked out in helping children
recall points from a meeting for Bible study:

'One evening we took a little boy with us who is
six years old and usually not very attentive at the
meetings. While going to the hall, I said: "Let's
play a game. On the way home let's see if we can
remember the songs sung and some of the main
points covered in the meeting." Going home we
were amazed. The youngest boy, who is usually in-
attentive, was given first chance to talk and he recalled many of the points. Our children then added
their comments and finally we two adults commented. Instead of work, it was fun to them.'

¹⁵ As a child grows older he will learn to express
ideas, draw things, do some work, play some music
on an instrument. He feels a sense of accomplishment. His work is, in a sense, an extension of
himself. It is very personal to him. If you look
at it and say 'Well done,' the child's spirits soar.
Find something in his work that you can sincerely
praise, and he will be encouraged. Criticize it

_____
15. How might a child be encouraged to better his accomplishments?

bluntly, and he will likely wilt and lose heart. Raise a question about a certain aspect of it if need be, but do not let it come as a rejection of his work. For example, rather than taking his own drawing and redoing it, you might demonstrate some improvement on another piece of paper. This allows him to adjust his own drawing if he wishes to. By encouraging his effort you encourage his growth; by harshly criticizing him, you may dishearten him or smother his desire to keep trying. Yes, the principle at Galatians 6:4 can also apply to children: "Let him prove what his own work is, and then he will have cause for exultation in regard to himself alone, and not in comparison with the other person." A child, especially for his first efforts, needs encouragement. If the project is good for his age, praise it! If it isn't, praise the effort, and encourage another try at it. After all, he didn't walk on his first try.

HOW SHOULD I EXPLAIN SEX?

[16] You answer your child's questions and encourage him to communicate. But then you are suddenly asked about sex. Do you answer frankly or do you give some misleading answer, such as saying that a little baby brother or sister was obtained at the hospital? Will you give correct information or let the children get poor, even wrong, answers, perhaps in an obscene context, from older children? The Bible contains frank references to quite a number of things relating to sex or the genital organs. (Genesis 17:11; 18:11; 30:16, 17; Leviticus 15:2) When instructing his people regarding gatherings where his Word was

---

16. In view of what the Bible says, what kind of answers should be given to a child's questions about sex?

to be read, God said: "Congregate the people, the men and the women and the little ones . . . in order that they may listen and in order that they may learn." (Deuteronomy 31:12) So the little children would hear any such references in a serious, respectful atmosphere, not in the form of "street talk."

[17] Really, the explaining of sex need not be as difficult as many parents imagine. Children become aware of their bodies very early, discovering the various parts. You name them for the child: hands, feet, nose, stomach, buttocks, penis, vulva. The little child is not embarrassed, unless you suddenly change and become "hush-hush" about the genital parts. What appalls parents is that they think they are going to have to explain everything, once the questioning starts. Actually, the questions come piecemeal, as the child reaches different stages of his development. As different stages are reached, you need only supply the proper vocabulary and very simple, general explanations.

[18] For example, one day you are asked, 'Where do babies come from?' You can just answer simply by saying something like: 'They grow inside their mothers.' Usually, that's all that is needed, for now. Later on your child may ask, 'How does the baby get out?' 'There's a special opening for it.' And that usually satisfies, for now.

[19] Some time later the question may come, 'How did the baby start?' Your answer may be: 'A father and a mother want to have a baby. A seed from the father meets an egg cell in the mother and a baby starts to grow, like a seed in the ground will grow into a flower or a tree.' So, it is

_____

17-19. How might explanations about sex be given progressively?

a continued story, each segment being sufficient to satisfy the child for the time being. Later the child may ask, 'How does the father's seed get into the mother?' You may simply say: 'You know how a boy is. He has a penis. The girl has an opening in her body that it fits into. The seed is planted. People are made that way so that babies can be started and grow in the mother, and finally come out as a baby.'

[20] This honest approach is certainly better than false stories or a "hush-hush" reaction that makes the subject seem like something distasteful. (Compare Titus 1:15.) It is also better for the child to hear the facts from its parents, who can accompany their explanations with reasons why babies should properly come only from married persons who love each other and who have accepted the responsibility to love and care for the baby. This puts the subject on a wholesome, spiritual plane, rather than its being learned in a setting that makes it all seem unclean.

TRANSMITTING LIFE'S MOST IMPORTANT LESSONS

[21] Jesus once likened people of his time to "young children sitting in the marketplaces who cry out to their playmates, saying, 'We played the flute for you, but you did not dance; we wailed, but you did not beat yourselves in grief.'" (Matthew 11:16, 17) The children's games were in imitation of grown-ups and their festivals and funerals. Because of the child's natural tendency to imitate, parental example plays a powerful role in a child's training.

---

20. Why is it good for parents to be the ones who give their children explanations about sex?
21. In view of what tendency in children is it important for parents to set a good example for their offspring?

[22] From the time of birth, your baby is learning from you—not just by what you say but *how* you say it, by the tone of voice you use in talking: to the baby itself, to your mate and to other persons. It observes parents' ways of dealing with each other, with other members of the family and with visitors. Your example in these things can begin to convey lessons far more vital than your child's learning to walk or to count or the ABC's. It can lay a foundation for the knowledge and understanding that lead to genuine happiness in living. That example can make the child receptive to the communication of righteous standards when it is old enough to be taught by speech and reading.

[23] "Become imitators of God, as beloved children, and go on walking in love," is the apostle's exhortation to Christians. Just before this, he showed what imitating God called for, saying: "Let all malicious bitterness and anger and wrath and screaming and abusive speech be taken away from you along with all badness. But become kind to one another, tenderly compassionate, freely forgiving one another just as God also by Christ freely forgave you. Therefore, become imitators of God, as beloved children . . ." (Ephesians 4:31, 32; 5:1, 2) If the voices that an infant hears, or the actions that it sees, convey lessons in irritability, as do loud and shrill talking, whining complaints, arrogance or explosive anger, an imprint is made that is hard to erase. If you are kind and considerate to all, if your moral standards are high and your principles are good, then your child will tend to imitate you in this. Act the way

---

22. What effect may the conduct of parents have on their children?
23, 24. If parents want their children to measure up to certain standards, what must they themselves be willing to do?

you want your children to act, be the way you want your children to be.

[24] Parents should not have two sets of principles, one to preach and the other to practice, one for their children and the other for themselves. What good is it to tell your children not to lie, if you lie yourself? If you break your promises to them, can you expect them to keep their promises to you? If parents are not respectful to one another, how can they expect their child to learn respect? If the child never hears his father or mother express humility, how can humility become his standard? A serious danger of a parent's conveying the idea of his being always right is that then the child may feel that everything the parent does is right—even when the parent does things that manifest an imperfect, sinful nature and are wrong. To say but not do is to be like the hypocritical Pharisees, of whom Jesus said: "All the things they tell you, do and observe, but do not do according to their deeds, for they say but do not perform." So, parents, if you do not want little Pharisees in your family, do not be big Pharisees!—Matthew 23:3.

[25] Children first learn about love by seeing it and they learn to give love by receiving it. Love cannot be bought. Parents may shower gifts upon their children. But love is primarily a spiritual matter, of the heart and not of the pocketbook, and gifts alone can never substitute for genuine love. To try to buy love cheapens it. More than material gifts, give of yourself, your time, your energy, your love. You will receive in like measure. (Luke 6:38) As 1 John 4:19 says about our love for God: "We love, because he first loved us."

---

25. How should children be taught about love?

²⁶ Children can learn about giving by receiving. They can be helped to learn the joys of giving, of serving, of sharing. Help them to see that there is happiness in giving—to you, to other children, to grown persons. Often adults do not want to accept gifts from children, mistakenly thinking it shows love to let the children keep for themselves the gifts they would give. One man stated:

> "I used to refuse when a child offered me some of his candy. I thought I was being kind, not taking what I knew he liked so much. But when I refused and let him keep it all for himself, I didn't see the joy I thought the child would show. Then I realized that I was rejecting his generosity, rejecting his gifts, and rejecting him. Thereafter I always accepted such gifts, to let him know the joys of giving."

²⁷ Parents in one family wanted to help their small son to become like those described in the Bible at 1 Timothy 6:18, "liberal, ready to share." So, when attending a place for Bible study they would take the money they were going to contribute and give it to their son, letting him drop it into the contribution box. This helped to impress upon him the value of giving support to spiritual matters and of helping to supply whatever material needs these may involve.

²⁸ Just as children can learn to love and be generous if right instruction is accompanied by good example, so too they can learn to apologize when it is appropriate. One parent said: "When I make a mistake with my children, I admit it to them. Very briefly I tell them why I made the

---

26, 27. How might children be taught the joy that comes from giving?
28, 29. How might children be taught the importance of apologizing for wrongs?

mistake and that I was in error. It makes it easier
for them to admit their mistakes to me, knowing
I'm not perfect and will understand." Illustrating
this viewpoint was an occasion when a stranger
was visiting a family and the father was introducing the family members to him. The visitor
commented:

> "All present were introduced, and then a smiling
> little boy came into the room. The father said, 'And
> this is our last son, the one with the jam on his
> shirt.' The boy's smile disappeared and a look of
> hurt came over his face. Seeing that embarrass-
> ment was about to bring tears, the father quickly
> pulled the child to him and said, 'I shouldn't have
> said that; I'm sorry.' The boy sobbed a moment,
> then left the room, but soon was back, with an
> even bigger smile—and he had a fresh clean shirt
> on."

[29] Certainly the bonds of affection are strengthened by such humility. Of course, later on a parent
can explain to a child how to take a balanced viewpoint of life's problems, big and small. He can aid
his children to learn not to view minor matters
too seriously, to be able to laugh at themselves
and never to expect perfection of others even as
they do not want it expected of themselves.

GIVE A SET OF TRUE VALUES

[30] Today many parents are confused as to what
the true values of life are. As a result, many children are never given a set of values. Some parents
even doubt their right to shape their children's
attitudes. If parents don't, other children, neighbors, movies and television will. Generation gaps,
youth revolts, drugs, new moralities and sexual
revolutions—all of this frightens parents. But the

30-32. Why is it vital for parents to start very early in helping
their children to recognize true values in life?

truth is, the child's personality is already quite developed before these issues begin to arise in its life.

[31] Studies reported on in one scientific journal say that "the major portion of the individual's personality is established before the onset of school. It is, of course, common knowledge that preschool children are extremely impressionable and malleable. . . . However, we have discovered that what they have encountered in their childhood in terms of attitudes and experiences often establishes lasting and sometimes immutable, behavior patterns."

[32] Wrong patterns can be changed, but another researcher explains what happens if precious years are allowed to slip by: "The child remains malleable during his first seven years, but the longer you wait, the more radically you need to change his environment—and the *probability* of change becomes a little less with each successive year."

[33] Small children have to learn many basic concepts, but those of greatest importance are the concepts of what is true and what is false, what is right and what is wrong. Writing to the Ephesian Christians, the apostle Paul urged them to gain accurate knowledge, saying, "We should no longer be babes, tossed about as by waves and carried hither and thither by every wind of teaching by means of the trickery of men, by means of cunning in contriving error. But speaking the truth, let us by love grow up in all things into him who is the head, Christ." (Ephesians 4:13-15) If parents are slow about helping little ones to develop a love

---

33. What are the most important concepts that children should be taught?

of truth and honesty, a love for what is right and good, the children will be left defenseless against error and wrong. The preschool years pass almost before parents realize it. Don't let them slip by; use those first few, vital, formative years with your children to give them a set of true values. You may save yourself heartache in later years. —Proverbs 29:15, 17.

[34] "The scene of this world is changing," wrote the inspired apostle, and that is certainly true of its material, emotional and moral standards. (1 Corinthians 7:31) There is little stability in the world. Parents must recognize that, being human, they too can fail in this regard. If they have their children's best interests at heart and are really concerned for their future happiness, parents will point their children to a set of standards that are truly stable. They can do this by impressing upon their children from infancy onward that, whatever question may arise, whatever problem needs solution, God's written Word, the Bible, is the place to turn to for answers that are decisive and most helpful. No matter how confusing or obscure circumstances may at times cause life to seem, that Word will continue to be 'a lamp to their feet, and a light to their roadway.'—Psalm 119:105.

[35] Yes, this is your period of golden opportunity to begin building in your children a set of values that can sustain them throughout their lives. No career is greater, no job more important, than training your children. The time to start is as soon as they are born, in their infancy!

---

34. Why are stable standards important, and what is the best source of such standards?
35. How important is the training of one's children?

The Value of Disciplining in Love

10

O BEDIENT, loving, well-mannered children do not just happen. They are molded and produced through example and discipline.

² Many child psychologists put a "hands off" sign on children, as did one who said: "Do you mothers realize that every time you spank your child you show that you are hating your child?" But in his Word, God says: "He who spares the rod hates his son, but he who loves him is diligent to discipline him." (Proverbs 13:24, *Revised Standard Version*) A few decades ago, particularly in Western nations, books on child training, with their theories of permissiveness, flooded the market. Discipline would inhibit the child and stunt its development, the psychologists said; and as for spanking, just the thought of it was horrifying to them. Their theories collided head on with Jehovah God's counsel. His Word says you 'reap what you sow.' (Galatians 6:7) What have a few decades of sowing the seeds of permissiveness proved?

³ The bumper crop of crime and delinquency is well known. Youth crime accounts for over 50 percent of serious crime in many industrialized

---

1. What is needed if one's children are going to be obedient?
2. How do the views of many child psychologists conflict with the Bible's counsel?
3, 4. What has resulted from a lack of proper discipline in the home, and so what do many recommend?

nations. In some parts of the world, school campuses are hotbeds of class disruptions, fights, verbal abuse and obscenities, vandalism, assault, extortion, arson, robberies, rapes, drugs and murders. A spokesman for a federation of teachers in one major country traced the discipline problem to the school's failure to reach the children at an early age, and blamed delinquency on the deterioration of the family and the unwillingness of parents to set reasonable standards of behavior for their children. In considering the question of 'why some members of a family become criminal while others do not,' *The Encyclopædia Britannica* says: "Family disciplinary policies may be either too lax, too severe, or too inconsistent. American research has suggested that unsound discipline may be related to about 70 percent of criminal men."

[4] The results experienced have led to a reversal of opinion among many and a return to discipline.

THE ROD OF DISCIPLINE

[5] A spanking may be a lifesaver to a child, for God's Word says: "Do not hold back discipline from the mere boy. In case you beat him with the rod, he will not die. With the rod you yourself should beat him, that you may deliver his very soul from Sheol [the grave] itself." Again, "Foolishness is tied up with the heart of a boy; the rod of discipline is what will remove it far from him." (Proverbs 23:13, 14; 22:15) If parents hold their children's life interests dear to them, they will not weakly or carelessly let disciplinary action slip from their hands. Love will motivate them to take action, wisely and fairly, when it is needed.

---

5. What is the Bible's view of spanking?

⁶ As regards discipline itself, it is not limited to punishing. Discipline basically means 'instruction and training that holds to a certain order or framework.' That is why Proverbs 8:33 says, not *'feel* discipline,' but *"listen* to discipline and become wise." The Christian, according to 2 Timothy 2: 24, 25, "needs to be gentle toward all, qualified to teach, keeping himself restrained under evil, instructing with mildness those not favorably disposed." The word "instructing" here is translated from the Greek word for discipline. The same word is so translated at Hebrews 12:9: "We paid due respect to the earthly fathers who disciplined us; should we not submit even more readily to our spiritual Father, and so attain life?"—*New English Bible.*

⁷ A parent who fails to provide discipline will not gain a child's respect, any more than will rulers gain the respect of citizens when they allow wrongdoing to go on with impunity. Discipline, rightly given, is evidence to a child that his parents care about him. It contributes toward a peaceful home, for "to those who have been trained by it it yields peaceable fruit, namely, righteousness." (Hebrews 12:11) Disobedient, badly behaved children are a source of irritation in any home, and such children are never truly happy, not even with themselves. "Chastise your son and he will bring you rest and give much pleasure to your soul." (Proverbs 29:17) After some firm but loving correction, a child can get somewhat of a new outlook and a fresh start and often is far more pleasant company. Discipline, indeed, "yields peaceable fruit."

6. What does discipline include?
7. What benefits result from discipline by parents?

[8] "Whom Jehovah loves he disciplines." (Hebrews 12:6) So it is with the parent who truly has his children's best interests at heart. Disciplining is to be done out of love. Anger may be normal when one becomes provoked by a child's wrongdoing, but, as the Bible shows, one should be "keeping himself restrained under evil." (2 Timothy 2:24) After a person has cooled down, a childish sin may not seem so big: "The insight of a man certainly slows down his anger, and it is beauty on his part to pass over transgression." (Proverbs 19:11; see also Ecclesiastes 7:8, 9.) There may be extenuating circumstances: Perhaps the child is overly tired or does not feel well. Maybe he actually forgot what he had been told; adults do that too, don't they? But even if some wrongdoing is not to be passed over, the discipline should not be an uncontrolled outburst or a blow that simply releases the emotional pressure of the parent. Discipline involves instruction, and by an angry outburst a child learns a lesson, not in self-control, but in the lack of it. The feeling of being cared for that the child senses in well-administered discipline is absent. Balance, then, is essential and promotes peace.

SETTING FIRM LIMITS

[9] Parents are to provide guidelines for their children. "Observe, O my son, the commandment of your father, and do not forsake the law of your mother. Tie them upon your heart constantly; bind them upon your throat. When you walk about, it will lead you; when you lie down, it will

8. How can parents discipline in love?
9. In harmony with Proverbs 6:20-23, what should parents provide for their children?

stand guard over you; and when you have waked up, it itself will make you its concern. For the commandment is a lamp, and a light the law is, and the reproofs of discipline are the way of life." These parental precepts are to guide and protect the child, and they reflect the parents' concern for the child's welfare and happiness.—Proverbs 6:20-23.

[10] A father who fails in this bears responsibility. Eli, a high priest in ancient Israel, let his sons indulge in greed, disrespect and immorality; he expressed some protest to them but took no real action to put a stop to their wrongdoing. God said: "I am judging his house to time indefinite for the error that he has known, because his sons are calling down evil upon God, and he has not rebuked them." (1 Samuel 2:12-17, 22-25; 3:13) Similarly, if a mother fails in her duty, she suffers disgrace: "The rod and reproof are what give wisdom; but a boy [or a girl] let on the loose will be causing [the] mother shame."—Proverbs 29: 15.

[11] Children need limits set for them. They are ill at ease without them. Having them and following them make the children feel part of a group; they belong to it and are accepted by it because they conform to its requirements. Permissiveness abandons the young and leaves them floundering on their own. The results show that children need adults who have firm convictions about limits, and who will pass these on. Children need to recognize that there are limits for everyone on earth and that this results in personal happiness

10. What can happen when parents fail to discipline their children?
11. Why do children need to have limits set for them?

and good. Freedom can be enjoyed only when others recognize our area of freedom and we recognize theirs. Overstepping proper limits inevitably means that the offender is going 'to the point of harming and encroaching upon the rights of his brother.'—1 Thessalonians 4:6.

[12] When children learn that defiance of proper limits brings discipline of one kind or another, they come to recognize their own limits, and through parental firmness and guidance they develop the self-discipline needed to live satisfying lives. Either we discipline ourselves from within, or we will be disciplined by some outside source. (1 Corinthians 9:25, 27) If we develop inner discipline and help our children to do the same, our lives and theirs will be happier, freer from troubles and heartaches.

[13] Guidelines and limitations for children should be clear to them, fair, and with merciful allowances. Expect neither too much nor too little. Remember their age, for they will act it. Do not expect them to be miniature adults. The apostle said that, when he was a babe, he acted like one. (1 Corinthians 13:11) But once reasonable rules have been established and your children understand them, enforce them promptly and consistently. "Let your word Yes mean Yes, your No, No." (Matthew 5:37) Children actually appreciate parents who hold to their word, who are consistent and predictable, for they sense their parents' strength supporting them and feel that they can rely on it when trouble comes and they need help. If their parents are fair yet positive in correcting

---

12. Why is self-discipline important, and how might parents help their children to develop it?
13. What are some important factors for parents to keep in mind when setting forth guidelines for their children?

wrongdoing, this gives children a feeling of security and stability. Children like to know where they stand, and with such parents they do know it.

[14] It takes determination on the part of parents to show firmness when a child balks at obeying a parental order. Some parents then resort to threats of possible punishment, engage in fruitless arguing with the child or turn to attempts at bribing the child to do what they have told it to do. Often all that is needed is simply to be very firm and to tell the child, with conviction, that he *must* do it and do it *now*. If a child were about to step in front of an oncoming car, parents would tell it what to do in no uncertain terms. As certain researchers on the subject point out: "Nearly all parents get their children to go to school, . . . to brush their teeth, to stay off the roof, to take baths, and so on. The children often resist. But they comply, nonetheless, because they know the parents mean business." You can expect your children to 'tie your guidelines and commandments upon their heart constantly' only if you reinforce these consistently.—Proverbs 6:21.

[15] When parents spasmodically enforce guidelines according to the whim or mood of the moment, or when discipline for disobedience is long delayed, children are emboldened to chance some violations to see how far they can go and how much they can get away with. When retribution seems to lag, children are like grown-ups in becoming bold in wrongdoing. "Because sentence against a bad work has not been executed speedily,

---

14. Why is firmness important when children do not respond to direction from their parents?
15. When parents are inconsistent in enforcing guidelines, how may the children be affected?

that is why the heart of the sons of men has become fully set in them to do bad." (Ecclesiastes 8:11) So, say what you mean, and mean what you say. Then your child will recognize that this is the case and will realize that neither pouting, arguing, nor acting as though he feels you are cruel and unloving, will be of any use.

[16] This requires thinking before speaking. Rashly made rules or commands are often unreasonable. "Be swift about hearing, slow about speaking, slow about wrath." (James 1:19) If discipline is not fair and consistent, the natural sense of justice that children possess will be offended, and resentment will develop.

KEEP ENTERTAINMENT UNDER CONTROL

[17] Play is a natural part of a child's life. (Zechariah 8:5) Parents must recognize this, while gradually introducing into the child's life an appreciation for work and a sense of responsibility. Then, whatever chores the child may come to have are generally best done first; play comes second.

[18] Some children become "street children" or virtual strangers at home due to seeking entertainment elsewhere. If the associations are poor, the effects will be poor. (1 Corinthians 15:33) Some association outside the home is, of course, beneficial to the child so as to develop a broadened understanding of people. But when there is too much outside association or it is left uncontrolled, the family circle becomes weakened or even fragmented.

---

16. To avoid giving unreasonable commands, what should parents do?
17. What view of work and play should children come to appreciate?
18. What effect can associates have on children?

[19] Along with the discipline they give to correct this, parents may well ask themselves what they might do to make the home more enjoyable for their children; whether they are spending enough time with them, not just in instructing or disciplining them, but also in being true friends and companions to their children. Are you usually "too busy" to spend time with your children, to play with them? Once they are missed, opportunities to do things with a child will not come back. Time is one-directional, and the child does not stand still but keeps growing and changing. Seasons flow by, and though it seems like just yesterday that your son was a baby learning to walk, you suddenly realize that he is becoming a young man, and your little girl has been transformed into a young lady. Only if you maintain a good balance and discipline yourself in your own use of time can you avoid slighting the opportunities this precious period offers—or prevent seeing your children draw away from you while yet in tender years.—Proverbs 3:27.

[20] Where television is a common source of recreation, limits may need to be set on its use. Some parents use TV as a baby-sitter. It may be convenient and seem to be cheap; but in reality it can prove very costly. Television programs are often saturated with violence and sex. The impression given is that violence is an acceptable way of solving problems; illicit sex appears as an acceptable part of everyday life. Many surveys have shown that this can desensitize a person to such

---

19. What are some things that parents might review to determine whether they are making the home an enjoyable place for their children?
20, 21. Where there is a television in the home, what responsibility should parents assume, and why?

practices, especially young persons. You are concerned that your children eat food that is healthful and not contaminated. You should be even more concerned about what their minds are being fed. As Jesus showed, food does not go into our hearts, but what we take into our minds may enter our hearts.—Mark 7:18-23.

21 Control over the kind of programs watched and also the amount of time spent in front of TV can make a big difference in a child's development. Television can provide some enjoyable entertainment and even education; but if uncontrolled it can become an addiction, consuming enormous amounts of time. Time is life, and some of that time could surely be spent in other more profitable ways. This is because television replaces *doing* with just *seeing*. It displaces not only physical activity, but also reading and conversation. A family needs communication and togetherness, and just sitting silently together in the same room watching television is not going to satisfy that need. Where an excess of TV watching is a problem, parents can develop in their children an appreciation for other activities in place of television—healthful play, reading, family activities— particularly if parents themselves take the lead and set the example.

WHEN YOU DISCIPLINE, COMMUNICATE!

22 One parent tells of this experience:

"When my son was just three years old I gave him quite a sermon on lying, how God hates liars, using Proverbs 6:16-19 and other scriptures. He listened and seemed to give the right responses. But I had a feeling he hadn't got the point. So I

22. Why is it important for children to understand the words used by their parents?

asked, 'Son, do you know what a lie is?' He said, 'No.' After that I always made sure he knew what the words meant and why he was being disciplined."

23 When children are still infants, parents may only be able to point things out as "no-nos," such as touching a hot stove. But even with those first simple warnings, reasons can be given. It may be simply that a stove is "hot!" and to touch it will "hurt!" From the start, however, keep before the child the principle that what is involved is for the child's good; then highlight the desirability of such qualities as kindness, considerateness and love. Help the child to appreciate that these qualities underlie all right requirements or restrictions. Also, emphasize why a certain action expresses these desirable traits or not. When this is done consistently, you may be able to reach not just the child's mind but his heart.—Matthew 7: 12; Romans 13:10.

24 Likewise, the need for obedience and respect for authority should be inculcated progressively. During the first year of life, a child's willingness or unwillingness to respond to adult demands will begin to show. As soon as the child's mental development allows for it, impress upon him an appreciation of the parents' responsibility to God. This can make a great difference in the child's response. Without this, children may view obedience as something they have to express merely because their parents are bigger and stronger than they are. If, instead, the child is helped to see that the parents are not giving their own ideas but are giving the child what the Creator says, what

23. What might be involved in helping children to see the rightness of a particular course of action?
24. Why is it important for a child to respect authority?

his Word says, this will give a strength to the parents' counsel and direction that nothing else can. It can be a real source of needed strength when rough areas begin to appear in a child's young life and he or she begins to feel the stress and strain of holding to right principles in the face of temptation or pressure.—Psalm 119:109-111; Proverbs 6:20-22.

[25] "The one covering over transgression is seeking love, and he that keeps talking about a matter is separating those familiar with one another." (Proverbs 17:9) This is true also in parent-child relationships. Once a child has been made aware of his mistake and understands why he needs to be disciplined, and the discipline has been given, love should move the parent to avoid harping on the transgression. Whatever was done, be sure you make clear that what you hate is the wrong, not the child. (Jude 23) The child may feel that he has 'taken his medicine' and may view frequent references to the incident as a needless humiliation. It could result in his alienation from the parents or other children in the family. If the parent is concerned that a wrong pattern is developing, then the matter can be dealt with later in some family discussion. Do not simply recite and review past acts, but consider instead the principles involved, how they apply and why they are so important to lasting happiness.

DIFFERENT WAYS TO DISCIPLINE

[26] "A rebuke works deeper in one having understanding than striking a stupid one a hundred

---

25. How might the counsel at Proverbs 17:9 help parents to discipline their children in the right manner?
26. Why do not all children respond in a desirable way to the same kind of discipline?

times." (Proverbs 17:10) Different children may need to be disciplined differently. The temperament and disposition of the individual child must be considered. One child may be very sensitive, and physical punishment, such as spanking, may not always be necessary. With another, spanking may be ineffective. Or a child may be like the servant described at Proverbs 29:19, one who "will not let himself be corrected by mere words, for he understands but he is paying no heed." In such a case the child would need corporal punishment.

[27] One mother reports:

> "My son was barely two when he wrote on the wall—little red marks not far from the floor. His father showed them to him and asked him about them. All he got was a big-eyed stare, not a Yes or a No. Finally his father said, 'You know, son, when I was about your age I wrote on a wall. It's kind of fun, isn't it?' Well, the little boy now relaxed, his face was all smiles, and he started an animated conversation about how much fun it was. He knew daddy understood! However, it was explained that even though it was fun, the walls were not the place for marking. Communication was established and, for this child, some further reasoning was all that was required."

[28] When disciplining, to give reasons so as to teach and instruct is fine, but it is not usually advisable to argue with a child. When her child argued about doing certain work, one mother simply said: "When you get it done we will go to the park," which was to be a treat for the youngster that day. Some pleasure or outing would be withheld until the assigned job was completed. If

---

27. How did one father help his little boy to stop marking on a wall?
28. How might a parent avoid arguing with a child?

she came to check and found the work was still undone, she would say, "Oh, not done yet? We'll go when you're through." She didn't argue, but she got results.

²⁹ Feeling the undesirable consequences of wrong acts can help children to learn the wisdom of right principles. Has a child made a mess? It may be that having to clean it up himself will make the strongest impression. Has he been unfair or rude? Learning to apologize may do the most to correct a wrong trend. He may have broken something in a moment of anger. If he is old enough, he might be required to earn money to replace it. With some children, the denial of certain privileges for a time may bring home the needed lesson. In the Christian congregation the withdrawal of friendly association is a way used to cause some wrong-doers to become ashamed. (2 Thessalonians 3:6, 14, 15) With youngsters, temporary banishment from family companionship can be more effective than spanking. Extremes, however, such as locking a child out of the house, go beyond what love would dictate. Whatever the method used, children need to be shown that they must bear the consequences of their behavior. This teaches them responsibility.

DISCIPLINE IN LOVE

³⁰ "Make sure of the more important things," keeping in mind that "the wisdom from above is . . . reasonable." (Philippians 1:10; James 3:17) Remember that young children are bundles of

---

29. What could be done to make a child feel the undesirable consequences of his wrongdoing?
30. Why is balance important when parents set guidelines for their children?

energy that is seeking release, and they are hungry to learn and explore and to try out new things. In setting out limitations and guidelines, show good judgment and be selective. There is a balance to be struck between what is essential and what isn't. Having made known the limits, then, rather than trying to control every minute detail, allow the child to enjoy moving freely and confidently within those limits. (Proverbs 4:11, 12) Otherwise your children may well become 'exasperated' and "downhearted," and you will find yourself worn out because of making issues of things that are not really of any particular consequence.—Colossians 3:21.

31 So, parents, "chastise your son [or daughter] while there exists hope," but do it God's way, in love. Imitate Him: "The one whom Jehovah loves he reproves, even as a father does a son in whom he finds pleasure." Make your discipline both valuable and loving, like your Creator's, for such "reproofs of discipline are the way of life." —Proverbs 19:18; 3:12; 6:23.

---

31. What example has Jehovah God set in giving discipline?

11

Keeping the Lines of Communication Open

COMMUNICATION is more than just talking. As the apostle Paul put it: If your words are not understood by the hearer, "you will, in fact, be speaking into the air." (1 Corinthians 14:9) Does what you say get through to your children, and do you really understand what they are trying to tell you?

[2] For true communication, there must be a transmitting of thoughts, ideas and feelings from one mind to another. If love may be called the heart of happy family living, then communication could be called its lifeblood. Breakdowns in communication between marriage mates spell trouble; they are equally serious, if not more so, when they come between parents and children.

TAKING A LONG-RANGE VIEW

[3] The greatest stresses on the lines of communication between parents and their children come, not during the early years of a child's life, but during adolescence—the "teen-age" years. Parents should recognize that this is going to be the case. It is unrealistic for them to expect that, because the earlier years of their children's lives are rela-

---

1, 2. What is communication, and why is it important?
3. During what period in a child's life should parents expect problems in communication?

tively trouble free, those later years will be also. Problems will definitely come, and clear, effective communication can be a key factor in solving or reducing them. Realizing this, parents need to look ahead, think ahead, for "better is the end afterward of a matter than its beginning."—Ecclesiastes 7:8.

[4] Many things go into establishing, building up and keeping family lines of communication operating. Over the years, a man and his wife can build up a depth of confidence, trust and mutual understanding that make communication possible even without words—just a look, a smile or a touch can speak volumes for them. They should aim to build up the same strong basis for communication with their children. Before a baby understands speech, parents communicate to it feelings of security and love. While the children are growing up, if the family works, plays and, more than that, worships together, then strong lines of communication are established. Keeping those lines open, however, calls for real effort and wisdom.

ENCOURAGING YOUR CHILD TO BE EXPRESSIVE

[5] The old saying is that "children should be seen and not heard." True—at times. Children need to learn that, as God's Word says, there is "a time to keep quiet and a time to speak." (Ecclesiastes 3:7) But children crave attention, and parents must guard against stifling free expression unnecessarily. Do not expect a small child's response to experiences to be the same as an adult's. The adult sees a single incident as just part of the

---

4. Must all family communication be in the form of conversation? Explain.
5-7. (a) Why is it good for parents to be careful about stopping a child from speaking? (b) How could parents teach children about politeness and courtesy?

broad panorama of life. The child may become very excited and so wholly absorbed in some matter of immediate interest that he forgets almost everything else. A small child may burst into the room and excitedly begin relating some event to his father or mother. If the parent cuts the child off with an irritated "Quiet down!" or makes some other angry expression, the child's enthusiasm may be crushed. Childish chatter may not seem to convey much. But, by encouraging natural expression from your children, you may prevent them later in life from keeping to themselves things that you want *and need* to know.

[6] Politeness and courtesy contribute to good communication. Children should learn to be polite, and parents should set the example for them in their own communication with the children, as well as in other ways. Reproof will be necessary and should be given when needed, even with severity. (Proverbs 3:11, 12; 15:31, 32; Titus 1: 13) However, if children are habitually cut off, continually corrected or, worse, disparaged and even ridiculed by a parent when they speak, they will likely become withdrawn—or they will go to someone else when they want to talk. The older the son or daughter grows, the more this becomes the case. Why not do this—at the end of this day stop and review your conversations with your son or daughter, and then ask yourself: How many times did I say things that expressed appreciation, encouragement, commendation or praise? On the other hand, how many times did I say things that implied the opposite, that tended to 'put him or her down,' that suggested dissatisfaction, irritation or exasperation? You may be surprised at what your review reveals.—Proverbs 12:18.

[7] Parental patience and self-control are frequently needed. Youths are inclined to be impetuous. They may blurt out what is on their minds, perhaps interrupting an adult conversation. A parent could bluntly rebuke a young one. But sometimes it may be wiser to listen politely, thereby furnishing an example of self-control and then, after answering briefly, kindly remind the child of the need to be polite and considerate. So, here again, the counsel may apply to be "swift about hearing, slow about speaking, slow about wrath."—James 1:19.

[8] You want your children to feel moved to seek your guidance when they have problems. You can encourage them to do that by showing that you also seek guidance in life and have someone to whom you look with submission. In commenting on a way he establishes good communication with his children while they are still small, one father said this:

> "Nearly every night I have prayers with the children at bedtime. They are generally in their bed, and I kneel beside it and hold them in my arms. I say a prayer and often they say one afterward. It is not uncommon for them to kiss me and say, 'Daddy, I love you,' and then reveal something that is in their heart. In the warmth of their bed and the security of their father's embrace they may tell of some personal problem they want help with or maybe just make an expression of affection."

At mealtimes and on other occasions, if your prayers are—not routine—but expressive, spoken from the heart and reflecting a genuine personal relationship with your heavenly Creator and Father, this can contribute immeasurably toward

---

8. How might parents encourage their children to come to them for guidance?

a wholesome relationship with your offspring.
—1 John 3:21; 4:17, 18.

THE TRANSITION YEARS

⁹ Adolescence is a time of transition, a time
when your son or daughter is no longer a child
but is not yet an adult. Teen-age bodies are under-
going changes, and these affect emotions. The
problems and needs of teen-agers differ from those
in the preteen period. So the parents' approach to
those problems and needs must be adjusted, for
what worked for the preteen-ager will not always
work for the adolescent. There is need for more
giving of *reasons,* and this calls for more, not less,
communication.

¹⁰ The simple explanations you gave to your
small child about sex, for example, will not meet
the needs of adolescents. They feel sex urges, but
embarrassment often keeps them from approaching their father or mother with questions. Parents
must take the initiative, and this will not be easy
unless they have built up and maintained good
lines of communication, particularly by being
warm companions of their children, in work and
play. The onset of seminal emissions for the boy
or menstruation for the girl will be less upsetting
if they have been explained beforehand. (Leviticus
15:16, 17; 18:19) A father may, perhaps while on
a walk with his son, bring up the matter of
masturbation, mentioning that most young men
have at least some problem with it, and ask, 'How
are you doing in that regard?' or 'Have you found
it to be a problem?' Even some family discussions

---

9. What can be said about the problems and needs of adolescents
when compared with those of younger children?
10. (a) Why are simple explanations about sex not sufficient for
adolescents? (b) How might parents get into discussions with
their child about sex?

can deal with related problems of adolescence, with both father and mother contributing their counsel in a relaxed but frank way.

UNDERSTANDING THE NEEDS OF TEEN-AGERS

[11] "Acquire wisdom; and with all that you acquire, acquire understanding." (Proverbs 4:7) As parents, be wise in the ways of the young; show insight as to their feelings. Do not forget how it was for you to be young. Remember, too, that while every older person was once young and knows what it was like, no young person has ever experienced being old. The adolescent youth doesn't want to be treated like a child anymore, but he is not an adult and does not have many adult interests yet. He still has a lot of play in him and needs some time for it.

[12] There are certain things that youths especially want from parents at this stage of life. They want to be understood; they want, more than ever, to be treated as individuals; they want guidelines and direction that are consistent and that take into account their approach to adulthood; they want very much to feel needed and appreciated.

[13] Parents should not be surprised because some measure of resistance to restrictions begins to surface in adolescence. This is due to the youths' approach to eventual independence and the normal desire for wider latitude of movement and choice. Helpless babies need constant parental care, small children need careful protection, but as they grow older the field of activity widens, and the ties with those beyond the family circle increase and

11. In what ways do adolescents differ from adults?
12. How do teen-agers want to be treated by their parents?
13. How might teen-age children react to parental restrictions, and why?

strengthen. The gropings toward independence may make a son or daughter somewhat difficult to deal with. Parents cannot let their authority be ignored or overruled—for their children's own good. But they can cope wisely and maintain communication if they keep in mind what motivates this possibly disturbing conduct.

[14] Confronted with their son's or daughter's urge for greater independence, what are parents to do? That urge is like a compressed spring held in the hand. Let it go suddenly and it will fly off uncontrolled in an unpredictable direction. Hold it in too long and you exhaust yourself and weaken it. But let it go gradually in a controlled way and it will stand in its proper place.

[15] We find an example of such controlled growth toward independence in the case of Jesus as a young lad. Of his preteen years, the historical account at Luke 2:40 says that "the young child continued growing and getting strong, being filled with wisdom, and God's favor continued upon him." His parents doubtless played a major role in his development, for, though he was perfect, his wisdom would not be automatic. They regularly provided the spiritual climate for his training, as the account goes on to relate. At the age of 12, while the family was in Jerusalem attending the Passover festival, Jesus went to the temple and engaged in conversation with the religious teachers there. Evidently his parents allowed their 12-year-old son this degree of freedom of movement. They departed from Jerusalem without realizing that he was being left behind, perhaps assuming

14. How might parents deal successfully with a child's desire for greater independence?
15. What shows that Jesus' growth to adulthood came under parental direction?

that he was with other returning friends or relatives. Three days later they found him at the temple, not trying to teach his elders but "listening to them and questioning them." His mother pointed out the mental anguish they had experienced and Jesus, with no disrespect, in effect replied that he thought they would surely know where to find him when they were ready to leave. Though he exercised some freedom of movement, the account says that Jesus thereafter "continued subject to them," adjusting to their guidelines and restrictions as he entered his teen years, and he "went on progressing in wisdom and in physical growth and in favor with God and men."—Luke 2:41-52.

[16] Similarly, parents should allow teen-age sons or daughters a degree of independence, gradually increasing it as they near adulthood, letting them make more and more personal decisions, under parental guidance and supervision. When difficulties arise, understanding why will help parents to avoid making great issues of minor things. Many times a teen-ager is not deliberately rebelling against his parents, but he is trying to establish a degree of independence without knowing how to go about it. So, the parents may make mistakes, perhaps making issues of the wrong things. If the matter is not too serious, let it pass. But when it is serious, be firm. Do not 'strain out gnats' nor 'swallow camels.'—Matthew 23:24.

[17] Parents can help the continuance of a fine relationship with their adolescent sons and daughters by showing good balance in the restrictions

---

16. When parents experience problems with an adolescent, what should they keep in mind?
17. What factors should parents take into consideration when placing restrictions on adolescent children?

they place on them. Remember that while the "wisdom from above is first of all chaste," it is also "reasonable" and "full of mercy," "not hypocritical." (James 3:17) There are some things that the Bible shows to be totally unacceptable, including stealing, fornication, idolatry and similar gross wrongs. (1 Corinthians 6:9, 10) With many other things, the rightness or wrongness may depend on the extent or degree to which a matter is carried. Food is good, but if we eat too much we become gluttons. So, too, with some forms of recreation, such as dancing, playing games, having parties, or similar activities. Many times it is not *what* is done, but the *way* it is done and the *company* in which it is done. So, just as we would not condemn eating when what we really mean is gluttony, parents would not want to make a blanket condemnation of some youthful activity if the real objection is to the extreme form or degree to which some carry it, or to some undesirable circumstances that could creep in.—Compare Colossians 2:23.

[18] All young people feel the need for having friends. Few may be considered "ideal," but, then, don't your own children have their weak points? You may want to restrict their associations with some young persons because of viewing these as potentially harmful. (Proverbs 13:20; 2 Thessalonians 3:13, 14; 2 Timothy 2:20, 21) With others, you may see some things you like and some things you do not like. Rather than excluding one completely because of some lack, you may want to express appreciation to your children for their friend's good qualities while pointing out the need for caution in the weaker areas, encouraging your

18. How might parents caution their children about associates?

son or daughter to prove a force for good in those areas, to the lasting benefit of the friend.

[19] One way to aid your teen-age son or daughter to develop a right view toward increased freedom is to help him or her see that greater responsibility goes with greater freedom. "To whom much was given, much will be demanded of him." (Luke 12:48) The more responsible children show themselves to be, the greater trust the parents can place in them.—Galatians 5:13; 1 Peter 2:16.

COMMUNICATING COUNSEL AND CORRECTION

[20] If a person counsels you but doesn't understand your position, you feel his counsel is unrealistic. If he has the power to force you to follow his demands, you may resent this as unjust. Parents should keep in mind that "the understanding heart is one that searches for knowledge," and "a man of knowledge is reinforcing power." (Proverbs 15:14; 24:5) You may have power over your children, but, if it is reinforced by knowledge and understanding, you will be more effective in communicating with them. Failure to show understanding when correcting young persons can lead to a "generation gap" and a breakdown of communication.

[21] What will you do if your child does get into difficulty, makes a serious mistake or commits some wrong that takes you by surprise? You should never condone the wrong. (Isaiah 5:20; Malachi 2:17) But realize that now of all times your son or daughter needs understanding help

19. In harmony with the principle set forth at Luke 12:48, how can children be helped to have the right view of freedom?
20. What besides power or authority over children is needed to prevent a breakdown of communication?
21. How should parents handle children who become involved in serious wrongdoing?

and skillful direction. Like Jehovah God, you may in effect say, 'Come and let us set matters straight; the situation is serious, but by no means beyond repair.' (Isaiah 1:18) Angry outbursts or harsh condemnations may throttle communication. All too many youths who go wrong have said: 'I couldn't talk to my parents—they would have been furious with me.' Ephesians 4:26 says: "If you are angry, do not let anger lead you into sin." (*New English Bible*) Hold your emotions in check while you hear what your son or daughter has to say. Then your fairness in listening will make the correction you give easier to accept.

²² Perhaps it is not just one incident but a period of difficulty, a pattern of manifesting some undesirable trait. Though discipline is essential, parents must never by word or spirit imply that they have given up on the child. Your long-suffering will be a measure of the depth of your love. (1 Corinthians 13:4) Do not combat evil with evil, but conquer it with good. (Romans 12:21) Only harm is done if a youth is humiliated before others by statements that he is "lazy," "rebellious," "good for nothing," or "hopeless." Love does not stop hoping. (1 Corinthians 13:7) A youth may go so far as to become delinquent and leave home. Though in no way expressing approval, parents can keep the way open for his return. How? By showing that they reject, not him, but his course. They can continue to express to him their belief that he has within him good qualities and their hope that these will win out. If that proves to be the case, he will, like the prodigal son of Jesus' illustration, be able to turn

---

22. Why should parents never imply that they have given up on their children?

homeward with the assurance that his repentant return will not be greeted with harshness or coldness.—Luke 15:11-32.

A SENSE OF INDIVIDUAL WORTH

[23] All human creatures need some recognition, to be accepted and approved, to feel that they belong. To get the acceptance and approval needed, of course, a person cannot become too independent. He must stay within the bounds of conduct approved by the group with which he belongs. Youths in their teens feel that need to belong in the family. Make them feel that they are valuable members of the family circle, contributing to its welfare, even being allowed to share in some of the family's planning and decisions.

[24] "Let us not become egotistical," says the apostle, "stirring up competition with one another, envying one another." (Galatians 5:26) Praise from a parent when a son or daughter does well will help to prevent such a spirit from rising; but comparing a youth unfavorably with someone else who is frequently held up as superior will create envy or resentment. The apostle said that each one should "prove what his own work is, and then he will have cause for exultation in regard to himself alone, and not in comparison with the other person." (Galatians 6:4) The youth wants to be accepted for what he himself is and for who he is and for what he is able to do, being loved by his parents for these things.

[25] Parents can help their son or daughter de-

---

23. Why is it important for adolescents to feel that they are valuable members of the family?

24. What should parents avoid doing so that one child does not become envious of another child?

25. How can parents aid their children to develop a sense of worth?

velop a sense of worth by training such a one to take on life's responsibilities in all areas. They have been training their children since infancy, in honesty, truthfulness and right treatment of others; they build on this earlier foundation by showing how these qualities apply in human society. How to take on the responsibility of a job and be dependable at it is included. Jesus, in his "progressing in wisdom" as a teen-ager, evidently learned a trade at his foster father Joseph's side, for even when he reached the age of 30 and began his public Kingdom work, people referred to him as "the carpenter." (Mark 6:3) During the teen-age period, boys especially should learn what it means to work and to satisfy an employer or a customer, even though the work be as simple in nature as running errands. They can be shown that by being diligent, serious and reliable workers they gain self-respect and the respect and appreciation of others; that not only are they a credit to their parents and family but they also "adorn the teaching of our Savior, God, in all things."—Titus 2:6-10.

[26] Daughters, too, can learn the arts of housekeeping and homemaking and earn appreciation and praise both inside and outside the family. A daughter's potential worth to her family is illustrated by the practice in Bible times of exacting a dowry or bride price when a daughter was given in marriage. This was doubtless viewed as a compensation for the loss of her services to the family. —Genesis 34:11, 12; Exodus 22:16.

[27] Opportunities for education should be used to

26. What ancient custom acknowledged that a daughter was a valuable member of the family?
27. Why should educational opportunities be used to good advantage?

good advantage to equip young ones for meeting life's challenges in the present system of things. Such young ones are included in the apostle's encouragement that "our people also learn to maintain fine works [honest employment, *New English Bible*] so as to meet their pressing needs, that they may not be unfruitful."—Titus 3:14.

THE PROTECTION OF THE BIBLE'S MORAL CODE

28 Parents are understandably concerned when circumstances, perhaps the neighborhood in which they live or the school their children attend, oblige these to associate with some youths who are delinquent and self-destructive. Parents may realize the truth of the Bible's statement that "bad associations spoil useful habits." They are therefore unwilling to accept the begging child's argument: 'Everyone else gets to do it; why can't I?' Probably not *everyone* is, but even so, it isn't reason enough for your child to do it if it is wrong or unwise. "Do not be envious of bad men [or children], and do not show yourself craving to get in with them. For despoiling is what their heart keeps meditating, and trouble is what their own lips keep speaking. By wisdom a household will be built up, and by discernment it will prove firmly established." —1 Corinthians 15:33; Proverbs 24:1-3.

29 You cannot trail your children through school or through life. However, by building up your household with wisdom you can send with them a good moral code and right principles for guidance. "The words of the wise ones are like oxgoads." (Ecclesiastes 12:11) In ancient times these goads were long sticks with pointed tips. They

---

28, 29. (a) What counsel does the Bible give about associations? (b) How can parents help their children to heed this counsel?

were used to prod the animals to keep moving in the right direction. Wise words of God will keep us moving the right way, and, if we stray, will cause our conscience to prick us to change our course. For your children's lasting welfare, send such wisdom along with them. Communicate it to them by both word and example. Instill a set of true values, and that is what your children will seek in others they choose as personal companions. —Psalm 119:9, 63.

[30] In all of this, remember that moral values are far more likely to be instilled if there is a home atmosphere in which those principles are respected and followed. Have the attitudes you want your children to have. In your own home, within the family circle, be sure that your children find adult understanding, love, forgiveness, a safe degree of freedom and independence along with justice and fairness, and the feeling of acceptance and belonging that they need. In these ways communicate to them a God-given moral code to take with them beyond the family circle. You can give them no finer heritage.—Proverbs 20:7.

---

30. How can parents provide their children with a God-given moral code?

12

Making Your Parents' Hearts Rejoice

WHETHER we are still very young, are moving into adulthood, or are now grown men and women, all of us are someone's children. It would be hard to estimate the worth of all the 20 years or so of care, work, money and self-sacrificing effort that have been expended on most of us from infancy to adulthood. And, in reality, our parents gave each of us something we cannot possibly give to them in return. For, whatever else we may owe them, we owe them our present life. Without them, we would not be. This obvious truth of itself should be more than enough reason for heeding the divine command: "'Honor your father and your mother'; which is the first command with a promise: 'That it may go well with you and you may endure a long time on the earth.'" —Ephesians 6:2, 3.

² While we are first indebted to our Creator as the true Source of all life, we should feel a deep sense of indebtedness to our parents. What can we give to them in exchange for what they gave us? God's Son said that all the world's possessions cannot buy life, for you simply cannot put a price tag on life. (Mark 8:36, 37; Psalm 49:6-8) God's

1. Why is it right to honor one's parents?
2. Why should we feel indebted to our parents?

Word tells us: "Do not you people be owing anybody a single thing, except to love one another." (Romans 13:8) In a special way, we should feel moved to keep giving love to our parents as something owed them as long as they and we live. While we cannot give them life as they gave it to us, we can contribute to them something that makes life worth living. We can contribute to their joy and their feeling of deep satisfaction. We can do that in a special way that possibly no other persons can, for we are their children.

[3] As Proverbs 23:24, 25 says: "The father of a righteous one will without fail be joyful; the one becoming father to a wise one will also rejoice in him. Your father and your mother will rejoice, and she that gave birth to you will be joyful." It is a natural desire of parents to be able to take pride in what their children do, to find pleasure in them. Is that the case with our parents?

[4] In large measure that depends on whether we genuinely respect their position and listen to their counsel. For those who are still young, God's counsel is: "Children, be obedient to your parents in everything, for this is well-pleasing in the Lord." (Colossians 3:20) "Everything" clearly does not mean that parents have authority to require things out of line with God's Word, but it does show that, while we are young, they are responsible to guide us in all aspects of life.—Proverbs 1:8.

[5] Are you now young? Someday you may be a parent. Would you want children who treated you

---

3. According to Proverbs 23:24, 25, what qualities in a child can contribute toward his parents' joy?
4. What does Colossians 3:20 direct children to do?
5. What might a young person ask himself as to what he would expect from children of his own?

with respect, or children who were defiant, perhaps who pretended to listen, but who disobeyed when out of your sight? Rather than bringing joy, Proverbs 17:25 says: "A foolish son is a vexation to his father and a bitterness to her who gave him birth." (*The Bible in Living English*) Just as you have a special ability to make your parents happy, you also, more than any other persons, can bring them deep sadness and disappointment. Your conduct will determine which way it will be.

ACQUIRING WISDOM TAKES TIME

⁶ It is good for youths to appreciate that age is an important factor in acquiring wisdom. Are you 10 years old now? You can see that you know more than when you were five, can't you? Are you 15? You know more than when you were 10, don't you? Are you approaching 20? You must appreciate that you know still more than when you were 15. It is easy to look back and see that age makes you wiser, but it is difficult to look ahead and accept this truth. No matter how wise a young person may feel, he or she should realize that the future can and should bring greater wisdom.

⁷ What is the point of this? That your parents, because they are older than you and have more experience than you do, reasonably are also wiser than you in coping with the problems of life. This is difficult for many young persons to accept. They may refer to older persons as "old fogies." Some may be, but many are not, no more than all young persons are irresponsible just because some are. It is not unusual for the young to think themselves

6. What illustration shows that wisdom usually comes with age?
7. What lesson about wisdom can we learn from the counsel given to King Rehoboam?

wiser than the old. A king of Israel made this blunder, with disastrous results. When 41-year-old Rehoboam succeeded his father Solomon as king, the people asked that their burdens be made lighter. Rehoboam consulted older men, who counseled gentleness and kindness. He then went to young men and they advised harsh measures. He took their advice. The result? Ten of the 12 tribes rebelled and Rehoboam was left with only about one sixth of his kingdom. The aged, not the young, gave the wise counsel. "Is there not wisdom among the aged and understanding in length of days?" —Job 12:12; 1 Kings 12:1-16; 14:21.

⁸ Do not consider the advice of your parents outdated just because they are no longer youths. Rather, as God's Word says: "Listen to your father who caused your birth, and do not despise your mother just because she has grown old." Age deserves respect. "Before gray hair you should rise up, and you must show consideration for the person of an old man, and you must be in fear of your God. I am Jehovah." True, many young people ignore these commands. But doing so has not brought happiness—not to themselves and certainly not to their parents.—Proverbs 23:22; Leviticus 19:32.

DO YOUR PART

⁹ There is no getting around it—what you do affects other people. If one member of the family suffers, all are disturbed. Also, if one is a complainer or a rebel, the peace of the entire family is disrupted. In order to have a happy family life,

---

8. What attitude toward older persons, including parents, does the Bible encourage?
9. How is a family affected when one of its members complains needlessly or rebels?

each one must do his part.—Compare 1 Corinthians 12:26.

[10] There are positive, constructive things that you can do. Parents work hard to care for the needs of the family. If you are young and living at home, you can help. Much of life is spent at work. Some people complain about it. But if you learn to do good work and to do it with a good motive, it will bring genuine satisfaction. On the other hand, a person who doesn't do his share but expects others to do everything for him never knows that satisfaction, and he is a source of irritation to others, as the Bible says, just like 'smoke in one's eyes.' (Proverbs 10:26; Ecclesiastes 3:12, 13) So, when chores are assigned to you at home, do them and do them well. And if you really want to bring pleasure to your parents, do some extras, without being asked. You will probably find *that* work the most enjoyable of all —because you did it simply out of your heart's desire to bring happiness to them.

[11] When people are impressed by a young person, they almost always want to know whose child he or she is. When young David demonstrated remarkable courage and faith, King Saul right away asked: "Whose son is the boy?" (1 Samuel 17:55-58) You bear your family's name. What you do and the kind of person you are will affect the way people view that name and the parents who gave it to you. There are so many ways you can bring honor to your parents—in your neighborhood and at school—by showing kindness, helpfulness, respect and friendliness to others. And

10. Why is it beneficial for children to learn to do good work?
11. How can a child's words or actions reflect favorably on his parents?

at the same time you thereby honor your Creator. —Proverbs 20:11; Hebrews 13:16.

¹² Your parents' happiness is bound up with your own. Their efforts at training you are aimed to give you a good start on the road of life. Cooperate with them and you will give them great pleasure, for they want the best for you. As the inspired writer expressed it: "My son, if your heart has become wise, my heart will rejoice." (Proverbs 23:15) If your parents recognize their responsibility before God to guide you in ways of true wisdom, help them to discharge that responsibility faithfully. "Listen to counsel and accept discipline, in order that you may become wise in your future." —Proverbs 19:20.

¹³ There may be times when you feel that your parents require too much of you or that the restrictions are too many. To achieve the right balance in matters of discipline is not easy. Someday, if you have a family, you may find that you face the same problem. If your parents restrict your association with certain youths, or guard you against the use of drugs, or limit your association to some extent with those of the opposite sex, stop and think how much better it is to have parents who discipline than to have ones who don't care! (Proverbs 13:20; 3:31) Heed their discipline. You'll benefit yourself and make their hearts rejoice.—Proverbs 6:23; 13:1; 15:5; Hebrews 12:7-11.

¹⁴ Of course, many situations that arise at home

---

12. Why is it good for children to cooperate with the efforts of their parents to train them?
13. What might help a child to have the right view of restrictions that are imposed by his parents?
14, 15. When problems arise among family members, the application of what Bible principles might help a child to preserve peace?

are not of your own making. But how you react influences the atmosphere of the household. The Bible counsels: "If possible, as far as it depends upon you, be peaceable with all men." (Romans 12:18) It is not always easy to do this. We are all different; we see things differently and react differently. There will be conflicting opinions and desires. Suppose the conflict is with your brother or sister. You may feel that the other person is being selfish. What will you do?

¹⁵ Some children would promptly shout an accusation and demand that one of their parents intervene. Or, they might take things into their own hands, shoving and hitting, in order to get their way. But an inspired proverb says: "The insight of a man certainly slows down his anger." (Proverbs 19:11) In what way? In that it causes him to consider extenuating circumstances. (Perhaps the act was not deliberate.) It makes him remember the many times when he himself has been in the wrong. (And how grateful he is for God's forgiveness!) It may also make him realize that, even if his brother or sister is in the wrong, it would still be wrong on his part to let his anger disrupt the peace of the entire household. Of a person with such insight, the proverb goes on to say: "It is beauty on his part to pass over transgression."—See also Colossians 3:13, 14.

¹⁶ Basically, what makes God-fearing parents rejoice is the same as what makes the heart of Jehovah rejoice. What makes them feel hurt is what makes him feel hurt. (Psalm 78:36-41) Parents who do not know the mind of Jehovah God

16. What course of conduct on the part of their children makes God-fearing parents rejoice?

may rejoice if their children become popular in the world, make a name for themselves, make lots of money, and so on. However, parents having Jehovah as their God know that this world and its desires are passing away but that "he that does the will of God remains forever." (1 John 2:15-17) So, what really makes them happy is to see their children obey their Creator, do his will and reflect his qualities. It is true that godly parents are happy when their children do well in their studies at school. But they are happier when their conduct at school and elsewhere reflects loyalty to God's standards and a desire to please him. And they are especially pleased when those children continue to find pleasure in Jehovah's ways right on up through their adult life.

RESPONSIBILITY TO CARE FOR PARENTS

¹⁷ Our concern for our parents should not cool off if we leave home when we have grown up. We want them to be happy throughout their lives. For many years they cared for our needs, often at considerable sacrifice to themselves. What can we do now to show that we are appreciative?

¹⁸ We can keep in mind the godly requirement: "Honor your father and your mother." (Matthew 19:19) We may be busy. But we need to realize that it means a great deal to our parents to hear from us and to have us visit them.

¹⁹ As the years pass, "honor" may be shown in other ways. If there is need for material help, show appreciation for all that they did for you, and also for Jehovah's righteous requirements. The apostle Paul wrote concerning those who are elderly: "If

---

17-19. How might adult sons and daughters show that they appreciate their parents?

any widow has children or grandchildren, let these learn first to practice godly devotion in their own household and to keep paying a due compensation to their parents and grandparents, for this is acceptable in God's sight."—1 Timothy 5:3, 4.

[20] The fact that "honor" to one's parents may include material support is clearly shown in the Scriptures. On one occasion the Pharisees had accosted Jesus and accused his disciples of violating traditions. Jesus countered: "Why is it you also overstep the commandment of God because of your tradition? For example, God said, 'Honor your father and your mother'; and, 'Let him that reviles father or mother end up in death.' But you say, 'Whoever says to his father or mother: "Whatever I have by which you might get benefit from me is a gift dedicated to God," he must not honor his father at all.' And so you have made the word of God invalid because of your tradition." —Matthew 15:1-6.

[21] By declaring that their money or property was "a gift dedicated to God" they were, according to tradition, freed of responsibility to care for their parents. But Jesus did not agree. And we today need to take this to heart. It is true that, as a result of "social welfare" in many lands, some needs of elderly parents may be cared for. But is the provision really sufficient? If not, or if there is no such provision at all, children who honor their parents will do what they can to fill any actual lack. Indeed, caring for one's aged parents who are in need is, as the apostle Paul said, an evidence of "godly devotion," of one's devotion to

---

20, 21. (a) According to Matthew 15:1-6, what does honoring one's parents include? (b) Is there something that would excuse a person from honoring his parents in this way?

Jehovah God himself, the Originator of the family arrangement.

²² We should never think, however, that if parents in their later years have suitable food, clothing and shelter, nothing more is required. They also have emotional and spiritual needs. They need love and reassuring attention, many times desperately so. All our lives we need to know that someone feels love for us, that we belong to someone, that we are not alone. Children should not turn away from their elderly parents, as to either their physical or emotional needs. "He that is maltreating a father and that chases a mother away is a son acting shamefully and disgracefully."—Proverbs 19:26.

²³ From youth on into adult life, children have an important place in the lives of their parents. Many children are a source of grief and disappointment. But if you respect your parents' position and listen to their counsel, if you express genuine love and affection for them, you can be a daily source of joy to their hearts. Yes, "give your father and your mother cause for delight, let her who bore you rejoice."—Proverbs 23:25, *New English Bible*.

------

22. What besides material things should we give to our parents?
23. How can a child be a source of joy to his parents?

13

The Later Years

IF OUR lives are not filled with some activity, physical or mental, we become bored. Life seems empty, and we become restless. This problem sometimes arises for married persons when their children grow up and leave home. For their past many years, life was filled with the responsibilities of parenthood. Now all this activity and the responsibility of raising a family suddenly come to an end.

² Besides that, as the years pass, physical changes begin to occur. Wrinkles appear, hair begins to turn gray, the hairline may recede, and aches and pains that were never noticed before manifest themselves. The fact is that we are getting older. Refusing to face the facts, some persons put forth frantic efforts to prove that they are just as young as they ever were. They suddenly become very active socially—rushing to parties or indulging heavily in sports. This flurry of activity provides something to do, but does it bring lasting satisfaction? Will it make a person feel genuinely needed so that his life has real meaning?

³ Recreation can, of course, be enjoyable. And in your later years of life you may find that you have time to do some things that could not be done when your children were young. But letting

1, 2. (a) What problems may arise after children leave home? (b) How do some try to deal with the problem of advancing age?
3. While recreation may be enjoyable, what should be avoided?

171

pleasure-seeking become the dominant concern can bring serious problems.—2 Timothy 3:4, 5; Luke 8:4-8, 14.

THE BEAUTY OF PROVING LOYAL

⁴ At this time of life not a few persons seem to feel that they have to prove that they are still attractive to the opposite sex. They may begin by flirting with someone at a social gathering or elsewhere. Men, especially, have "affairs" with younger women, and in this time of the "new morality" there are also many women who seek reassurance by having extramarital "affairs." Although perhaps married for many years, some begin to nourish ideas about starting a "new life" with a new marriage mate. They may try to justify what they are doing by pointing to the faults of their mate—while generally making light of their own shortcomings, including their lack of loyalty, both to their mate and to righteous principles.

⁵ They may know that Jesus said: "Whoever divorces his wife, except on the ground of fornication [*porneia:* gross sexual immorality], and marries another commits adultery." Although Jesus was here showing that it is not right to divorce one's mate on "every sort of ground," they are willing to use any ground for divorce that secular laws allow. (Matthew 19:3-9) Then they proceed to get a new mate, often someone with whom they were involved before divorce proceedings ever began. While knowing what God's Word says about such conduct, they may reason that in his great mercy God will "understand."

4, 5. What can result when an older person feels that he has to prove he is still attractive to the opposite sex?

⁶ To avoid being enticed by such immoral thinking, we do well to consider what Jehovah, by means of his prophet Malachi, said to the people of Israel: " 'This is the . . . thing that you people do, this resulting in covering with tears the altar of Jehovah, with weeping and sighing, so that there is no more a turning [with approval] toward the gift offering or a taking of pleasure in anything from your hand. And you have said, "On what account?" On this account, that Jehovah himself has borne witness between you and the wife of your youth, with whom you yourself have dealt treacherously . . . And you people must guard yourselves respecting your spirit, and with the wife of your youth may no one deal treacherously. For he has hated a divorcing,' Jehovah the God of Israel has said." (Malachi 2:13-16) Yes, treachery in dealing with one's marriage mate, disrespect for the marriage covenant—these are condemned by God; they damage one's relationship with the Life-Giver.

⁷ Is this the way to a better life? Hardly. Any new marriage entered into by such persons rests on shaky ground. For one thing, they have shown that, even in this most precious relationship, they could not be counted on. True, they may see something appealing in the personality of the new mate that the former one did not have. But to get this, they sought their own pleasure regardless of causing hurt and heartache. Surely this is not a quality that works toward marital happiness.

⁸ The beauty of remaining true to a marriage

6. How does Jehovah God view disrespect for the marriage covenant?
7. Why does disrespect for the marriage covenant not lead to happiness?
8. In marriage, what is more valuable than physical beauty?

mate far surpasses any physical beauty. Physical beauty inevitably fades with the years, but the beauty of loyal devotion grows with each passing year. To seek another person's happiness, and to be willing to put his or her interests ahead of your own, can bring lasting satisfaction, for there really is "more happiness in giving than there is in receiving." (Acts 20:35) If two persons have been married for a number of years, and if they have communicated with and confided in each other, if they have shared work and goals and hopes, the hard times with the good—and have done this out of love—their lives will be genuinely united, interlaced. They have very much in common—mentally, emotionally and spiritually. The romantic love that may have blinded them somewhat to each other's faults before marriage will give way to a heartfelt devotion that causes each one to see the shortcomings of the other as an opportunity to be of help, to fill a need. Between them there is a feeling of genuine trust, a sense of security, knowing that they will stay by each other no matter what problems may arise. For them it seems only the natural thing to be loyal to each other. As Micah 6:8 states: "He has told you, O earthling man, what is good. And what is Jehovah asking back from you but to exercise justice and to love loyal love and to be modest in walking with your God?"—*Marginal reading.*

GROWN-UP CHILDREN—A NEW RELATIONSHIP

⁹ Although husband and wife are to remain

9-11. (a) Is it God's purpose for the relationship of parents and their children to remain identical throughout life? (b) What bearing does this have on the advice that parents may give to their grown children? (c) When their children are married, whose headship should parents respect?

together throughout life, that is not the Creator's arrangement for parents and their children. It is true that when your children were growing up they needed you every day. Not only were there physical needs that had to be cared for, but guidance was required. When they did not readily respond, you may have insisted on certain things that were for their own good. But when they establish their own household, the relationship between you and them changes to some extent. (Genesis 2:24) This does not mean that your feelings toward them change, but that there is a shifting of responsibility. So the way in which you do things for them needs to change.

[10] At times they may still need advice. And it is an evidence of wisdom if they listen to sound advice from those who have more experience in life. (Proverbs 12:15; 23:22) But when offering counsel to sons or daughters who are on their own, it is wise to do it in a way that shows you recognize the fact that decisions now rest with them.

[11] This is very important if they are married. There are some countries where long-established custom places the bride under the supervision of her mother-in-law. Elsewhere, in-laws exert strong influence in family affairs. But does this really result in happiness? The Creator of the family knows what is best, and he says: "A man will leave his father and his mother and he must stick to his wife." (Genesis 2:24) The responsibility for decisions now rests, neither with the parents of the husband nor with the parents of the wife, but with the husband. "A husband is head of his wife as the Christ also is head of the congregation," God's Word says. (Ephesians 5:23) Plea-

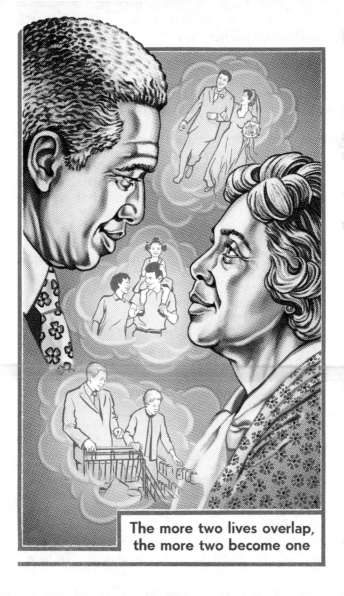

The more two lives overlap,
the more two become one

sure in doing things for your grown children, and later for your grandchildren, can be greatly enhanced when there is respect for this arrangement.

ENJOY DOING THINGS FOR OTHERS

[12] There is a need that all of us have to feel that our lives are useful, that they have meaning. Satisfying this need is important to your own well-being. Apart from your children, there are many others in whose lives you can help to fill a need. What about your own marriage mate? While your children were growing up, much of your attention was directed to them. Now you have opportunity to do more things in a personal way for each other. This can help to deepen your relationship. But why limit your kind deeds to your own household? You can 'broaden out' by giving assistance to neighbors who become ill or by sharing time with elderly ones who are lonely or by providing material aid, in whatever ways you can, to persons who through no fault of their own come into material need. (2 Corinthians 6: 11, 12) The Bible tells us of Dorcas, a woman who gained great love because she "abounded in good deeds and gifts of mercy that she was rendering" on behalf of widows. (Acts 9:36, 39) It commends those who are kind to the afflicted ones. (Proverbs 14:21) The Scriptures include 'looking after orphans and widows in their tribulation' as a vital part of the worship that is pleasing to God. (James 1:27) And the Bible encourages all of us: "Do not forget the doing of good and the sharing of things with others, for with such sacrifices God is well pleased."—Hebrews 13:16.

---

12. (a) After their children establish homes of their own, how might parents deepen their love for each other? (b) What else might they do to make their lives more meaningful?

[13] Does this mean that becoming engrossed in purely humanitarian activities is the key to happiness? Actually, unless the motivation is a spiritual one, a desire to imitate God in showing love, it can lead to frustration. (1 Corinthians 13:3; Ephesians 5:1, 2) Why? Because there may well be disappointments when persons do not appreciate your kindness or when they try to take unfair advantage of your generosity.

[14] On the other hand, when a person is truly using his life in the service of God, his greatest satisfaction comes from knowing that what he is doing is well pleasing to his Creator. And his ability to do things for other people is not limited by material resources. He has "the glorious good news of the happy God," Jehovah, and the privilege of sharing it with others. (1 Timothy 1:11) From the Bible he knows how to cope with the problems of life now, and what the grand hope that God holds out for the future is. And what a pleasure it is to share such good news with others, and then to draw their attention to the Source of it, Jehovah God! As the inspired writer of Psalm 147:1 said: "Praise Jah, you people, for it is good to make melody to our God; for it is pleasant—praise is fitting."

[15] It is when we understand Jehovah's will in connection with life and when we honor him that our own lives become filled with meaning. (Revelation 4:11) Genuine satisfaction will be yours if, to the extent that your circumstances permit, you participate fully in sharing Bible truths with other people. Although your own children may be grown, you can enjoy aiding 'spiritual children' to grow.

---

13. What motivation makes helping others worth while?
14, 15. What makes life truly happy and satisfying?

And as you see them develop into mature Christians, you will feel as did the apostle Paul when he wrote to some that he had thus assisted: "What is our hope or joy or crown of exultation—why, is it not in fact you? . . . You certainly are our glory and joy."—1 Thessalonians 2:19, 20.

BE FLEXIBLE WHEN CIRCUMSTANCES CHANGE

[16] In time, of course, most people find that they are no longer able to do as much as they once did. They need to be flexible, to be willing to make adjustments. Where there are health problems, these require attention. But it is wise to be balanced, not becoming so engrossed in these matters that one fails to see the opportunities that each day of life affords. Problems will exist, and if there is something constructive that one can do about them, it is wise to do it. But worry accomplishes nothing, and wishing that things were different does not change them. So, instead of longing for the past, take hold of the opportunities of the present.

[17] The same applies if, in later years of life, you again find yourself in the single state. If you had a happy marriage, you no doubt will cherish fond memories. But life goes on, and this is a time when adjustments are needed. There are new challenges to be met, and if you live in a way that demonstrates faith in God, you will not be alone in meeting them.—Psalm 37:25; Proverbs 3:5, 6.

[18] Despite life's unpleasant aspects, there is much that can bring us pleasure—fine friends,

---

16, 17. (a) When it comes to problems, what should be avoided? (b) Even if a person loses his mate in death, what can help him not to be alone in facing new challenges?
18-20. What factors can make life meaningful even in later years?

opportunities to do things for other people, the enjoyment of a good meal, a gorgeous sunset, the singing of birds. Furthermore, while our present circumstances may not be ideal, we have God's assurance that he will bring an end to wickedness and will remove from mankind all sorrow, anguish, sickness and even death itself.—Revelation 21:4.

[19] It is true that the person who has taken a largely materialistic view of life may find his later years very empty. The writer of Ecclesiastes described the results of such living by saying: "Everything is vanity." (Ecclesiastes 12:8) But concerning men of faith, such as Abraham and Isaac, the Bible says that they reached the end of their lives "old and satisfied." (Genesis 25:8; 35:29) What made the difference? These men had faith in God. They were convinced that in God's due time the dead would live again, and they looked forward to the time when God himself would establish a righteous government for all mankind.—Hebrews 11:10, 19.

[20] In your situation, too, if you do not allow the problems of the present to blind you to the many good things around you and the marvelous future that God has in store for his servants, your life will have meaning, and each day will bring you satisfaction, right on through the later years.

14

Building as a Family for an Eternal Future

TIME keeps on moving. The past may hold many fond memories for us, but we cannot live in the past. We can learn from the past, including past mistakes, but we can live only in the present. And yet, even though a family may be getting along well at present, the fact must be faced that the present is only momentary; today soon becomes yesterday, and the present quickly becomes the past. So, it is vital to family happiness that we keep looking to the future, preparing for it, planning for it. What it will be like, for us and those close to us, will depend to a large extent on the decisions we make now.

[2] What are the prospects? For the majority of mankind, what thoughts they have for the future often extend only a few short years. Many prefer not to look very far toward the future because all they can foresee is an unpleasant ending, with the family circle being broken by death. For many, their moments of happiness are quickly overshadowed by the anxieties of life. But by listening to the One "to whom every family in heaven and

---

1. In promoting family happiness, why is it good to think about the future?
2. (a) Why do many persons not want to think about the future? (b) If we desire a happy future, to whom should we listen?

on earth owes its name," there can be much, much more to life.—Ephesians 3:14, 15.

[3] When the first human pair were created, it was not God's purpose that they or their future children would live for just a few troubled years and then die. He gave them a paradise home and set before them the prospect of unending life. (Genesis 2:7-9, 15-17) But they forfeited that prospect for themselves and their offspring by deliberately violating the law of God, the One on whom their lives depended. The Bible explains it this way: "Through one man [Adam] sin entered into the world and death through sin, and thus death spread to all men because they had all sinned."—Romans 5:12.

[4] God, however, lovingly made provision to redeem the human family. His own Son, Jesus Christ, laid down his perfect human life in behalf of all the offspring of Adam. (1 Timothy 2:5, 6) Jesus thus purchased back or redeemed what Adam had lost for us, and the way was opened for those who would exercise faith in this provision to have the same opportunity for life that God had set before the first human pair. Today, if not overtaken by serious illness or accident earlier in life, a person may live for 70 or 80 years, and a few live a little longer. "But the gift God gives is everlasting life by Christ Jesus our Lord."—Romans 6:23.

[5] What can this mean for your family? For per-

3. (a) What prospects did God put before the first humans? (b) Why did things turn out differently?
4. What arrangement has Jehovah God made so that his original purpose regarding humankind will be realized?
5-7. (a) If we do God's will now, to what can we look forward in the future? (b) What question might you raise about helping your family?

sons who listen to and obey God's commandments it can mean an eternal future. (John 3:36) In his unfailing Word, God promises that he will remove the present oppressive system of things and cause all the affairs of mankind to be administered by a perfect and righteous government that he himself provides. (Daniel 2:44) Showing this, his Word tells us that he purposed "to gather all things together again in the Christ, the things in the heavens and the things on the earth." (Ephesians 1:10) Yes, then there will be universal harmony, and the human family will be united earth wide, free from racial strife, political division, heartless crime and the violence of war. Families will dwell in security, "and there will be no one making them tremble." (Psalm 37:29, 34; Micah 4:3, 4) This will be because all those then living will be persons who have "become imitators of God, as beloved children," and they will "go on walking in love."—Ephesians 5:1, 2.

⁶ Under the direction of God's Kingdom rule, the human family will then work unitedly in the joyful project of bringing the earth to the paradise state that the Creator purposed, a garden home providing an abundance of food for all mankind. All earth's immense variety of bird, fish and animal life will come under the kind dominion of humans and serve to their pleasure, for this is God's stated purpose. (Genesis 2:9; 1:26-28) No more will disease, pain, the debilitating effects of old age, or the fear of death mar the human family's enjoyment of life. Even those "in the memorial tombs" will return to share in the grand opportunities that life will then afford.—John 5:28, 29; Revelation 21:1-5.

⁷ What can you do to help your family realize the fulfillment of these prospects?

WHAT DO WE NEED TO DO?

⁸ None of us should mistakenly conclude that simply by living what we view as a "good life" we will be among those who gain life in God's new system of things. It is not for us to decide what the requirements are; God rightly does that. One day when Jesus was teaching in Judea, a man asked: "By doing what shall I inherit everlasting life?" The answer was: " 'You must love Jehovah your God with your whole heart and with your whole soul and with your whole strength and with your whole mind,' and, 'your neighbor as yourself.' " (Luke 10:25-28) Clearly, much more is involved than just saying that we believe in God, or periodically going to meetings where the Bible is discussed, or occasionally doing kind things for certain persons. Rather, the faith that we profess should deeply influence our thoughts and desires and actions every day, all day long.

⁹ Keeping in mind and treasuring our relationship with God will help us to act with wisdom and will assure his approval and help. (Proverbs 4:10) By viewing all the affairs of life as they relate to him and his purposes, we will be able to keep good balance in the way we use our lives. We must work to care for our physical needs. But God's Son reminds us that anxious concern and eager pursuit of material things will not lengthen our lives in the slightest; seeking first God's kingdom and his righteousness will lengthen them unending-

---

8. To gain God's approval, what is required of us?
9. What Scriptural principles can help us to be balanced in our view of the common affairs of life?

ly. (Matthew 6:25-33; 1 Timothy 6:7-12; Hebrews 13:5) God purposes that we thoroughly enjoy our family life. Yet to become so wrapped up in family affairs that we fail to show genuine love for those outside the family circle would be self-defeating, would give our family a narrow outlook on life and would rob us of God's blessing. Family fun and recreation bring the greatest enjoyment when they are kept in their place, never being allowed to crowd love for God into the background. (1 Corinthians 7:29-31; 2 Timothy 3:4, 5) By doing all things, as a family or as individuals, in harmony with the sound principles of God's Word, our lives will be deeply satisfying, with a sense of genuine accomplishment, and we will be laying a sound foundation for an eternal future. So, "whatever you are doing, work at it whole-souled as to Jehovah . . . for you know that it is from Jehovah you will receive the due reward of the inheritance." —Colossians 3:18-24.

BUILDING AS A FAMILY

¹⁰ If the members of a family are to continue to work toward the same goals, home discussions of God's Word are very valuable, really essential. Each day offers many opportunities for a person to relate to the purposes of the Creator things that are seen and done. (Deuteronomy 6:4-9) It is good to set aside regular times for all to join in reading and discussing the Bible together, perhaps with the help of publications that explain the Bible. Doing this has a unifying effect on the family. Family members can then use God's Word to help one another to cope with problems that

---

10. How important is regular Bible discussion in the home?

may come up. When parents set a good example, not letting such periods of family Bible discussion be easily infringed upon by other interests, this impresses upon the children the vital importance of deep respect and appreciation for God's Word. His Son said: "Man must live, not on bread alone, but on every utterance coming forth through Jehovah's mouth."—Matthew 4:4.

[11] In a body, "there should be no division," but "its members should have the same care for one another." (1 Corinthians 12:25) That should be true of a family body. One mate should not be so preoccupied with his own spiritual progress in knowledge and understanding that he fails to show sincere concern for that of his marriage partner. If, for example, a husband does not give sufficient attention to his wife's spiritual needs, in time she may no longer cherish the same goals that he does. If parents do not take enough personal interest in the spiritual growth of their children, helping them to see how the principles of God's Word apply and can bring the greatest happiness in life, they may find that the hearts and minds of their children will be drawn away by the materialistic spirit of the world around them. For the everlasting good of your whole family, keep the taking in of knowledge from God's Word as a regular, vital part of your family life.

[12] If, indeed, 'love begins at home,' it should not end there. God's Word foretold that his true servants would become, even during the present system of things, a global family of brothers and

---

11. When it comes to spiritual progress, what tendency should be avoided in the family?
12. With whom should we not neglect to associate?

sisters. He tells us that "as long as we have time favorable for it," we should "work what is good toward all, but especially toward those related to us in the faith," those in the "entire association of [our] brothers in the world." (Galatians 6:10; 1 Peter 5:9) As a family, meeting together regularly with those of that bigger "family" should be a joy, one not easily forfeited in favor of other interests.—Hebrews 10:23-25; Luke 21:34-36.

¹³ But our love should not be limited just to those already within "God's household," his congregation. (1 Timothy 3:15) As God's Son said, if we love only those loving us, our brothers only, 'what extraordinary thing have we done?' To be like our heavenly Father, we must reach out wholeheartedly to all persons and show kindness and helpfulness to any and all, seeking ever to share the good news of God's kingdom with them, taking the initiative. When we express godly love in this way as a family, our life takes on real meaning and purpose. All of us, parents and children alike, experience what it means to show love to its full extent, in the way that God shows it. (Matthew 5:43-48; 24:14) We also share in the full happiness that only such wholehearted giving can bring.—Acts 20:35.

¹⁴ What grand prospects are ahead for families who manifest such love! They have learned that the way to make their family life happy is to apply the counsel of God's Word. Despite the problems and pressures of life that affect all persons, such families experience right now many

13. What responsibility do we have toward persons outside the Christian congregation?
14. The application of what counsel promotes happy family life?

fine results from doing so. But they are looking beyond the present, and they are not thinking in terms of just a few years of life before death ends it all. With confidence in the reliability of the promises of God, each member of the family will happily build for an eternal future.

[15] This book has shown from the Bible that God's purpose in creating the earth is to have it inhabited. He established the family to accomplish this. Jehovah God also gave guidelines for fathers, mothers and children, and these have been considered. Have you been able to apply some of these principles in your family? Have they helped you to make your family life happier? We hope so. But what does the future hold for you and your family?

[16] Would you like to help in caring for the earth, in making its fields produce bumper crops and its deserts to blossom? Would you like to see thorns and thistles give way to orchards and majestic forests? Would you and your family be pleased to exercise dominion over animals, not with guns, whips and steel bars, but through love and mutual trust?

[17] If your heart yearns for the time when swords will be beaten into plowshares and spears into pruning shears, when there will be no more makers of bombs or fomenters of war, then you would rejoice in Jehovah's new system of things. Oppressive political rule, commercial greed and religious hypocrisy will be things of the past. Every family

---

15. What questions might you ask yourself about the benefits of the Scriptural guidelines set forth in this book?
16-18. What grand conditions has Jehovah God purposed for this earth?

will dwell in peace under its own vine and fig tree. The earth will ring with the happy cries of resurrected children and with the stirring songs of many birds. And the air will be exhilarating with fragrance of flowers instead of stifling with industrial pollution.—Micah 4:1-4.

¹⁸ If it is your heartfelt hope to see the lame leap like the stag, to hear the tongue of the mute sing, to watch the eyes of the blind open, to learn that the ears of the deaf are unstopped, to witness sighing and crying give way to smiles, and tears and mourning give way to laughter, and pain and death give way to health and eternal life, then do your utmost to aid yourself and your family to take the action needed to live forever in Jehovah's new system where such conditions will exist forever.—Revelation 21:1-4.

¹⁹ Will your family be among the happy throngs who will fill the earth at that time? It is up to you. Follow Jehovah's instructions for family life now. Work as a family to prove now that you would fit into the life-style of that new system. Study God's Word, apply it in your lives, tell others of the hope ahead. By so doing, you as a family will be making "a good name" with God. "A good name is to be chosen rather than abundant riches; favor is better than even silver and gold." Such a name Jehovah will not forget: "The remembrance of the righteous one is due for a blessing." (Proverbs 22:1, *margin;* 10:7) By Jehovah's undeserved kindness you and your family may be blessed with an eternal future of supreme happiness.

---

19. How may you and your family be among those who will enjoy the blessings of God's new system?

Other Aids for Your Family

Would you like other valuable aids for your family? You may obtain either one of the following by writing to Watch Tower, using the appropriate address on the next page.

● **Listening to the Great Teacher.** This book is also designed for young children. It employs teaching methods that draw children and parents together and makes learning a pleasure. The principal objective of this book is to teach children the Bible's high moral standards. By instructing young ones in right principles of living, you will really help them to cope with present-day problems. Delightfully illustrated, large print, easily understood wording, hardbound, pocket-size, 192 pages.

● **Questions Young People Ask—Answers That Work.** This book will help teenagers to counteract the immoral influences of today's world. Dishonesty, alcohol and drug abuse, sexual morality, dating and courtship are some of the subjects under discussion. Hardbound, 320 pages.

Would you welcome more information or a free home Bible study?

Write Watch Tower at appropriate address below.

ALASKA 99507: 2552 East 48th Ave., Anchorage. **ALBANIA:** Kutia Postare 3, Tiranë. **ARGENTINA:** Elcano 3820, 1427 Buenos Aires. **AUSTRALIA:** Box 280, Ingleburn. N.S.W. 2565. **AUSTRIA:** Postfach 67, A-1134 Vienna [13 Gallgasse 42-44, Vienna]. **BAHAMAS:** Box N-1247, Nassau, N.P. **BARBADOS:** Fontabelle Rd., Bridgetown. **BELGIUM:** rue d'Argile-Potaardestraat 60, B-1950 Kraainem. **BELIZE:** Box 257, Belize City. **BENIN, REP. OF:** BP 06-1131, Cotonou. **BOLIVIA:** Casilla No. 1440, La Paz. **BRAZIL:** Caixa Postal 92, 18270-000 Tatuí, SP. **BULGARIA:** P.K. 353, Sofia 1000. **CANADA:** Box 4100, Halton Hills (Georgetown), Ontario L7G 4Y4. **CENTRAL AFRICAN REPUBLIC:** B.P. 662, Bangui. **CHILE:** Casilla 267, Puente Alto [Av. Concha y Toro 3456, Puente Alto]. **COLOMBIA:** Apartado Aéreo 85058, Bogotá 8, D.E. **COSTA RICA:** Apartado 10043, San José. **CÔTE D'IVOIRE (IVORY COAST), WEST AFRICA:** 06 B P 393, Abidjan 06. **CROATIA:** p.p. 417, 41001 Zagreb. **CYPRUS:** P. O. Box 33, Dhali, Nicosia. **CZECHIA:** pošt. př. 65, 140 00 Praha 4. **DENMARK:** Stenhusvej 28, DK-4300 Holbæk. **DOMINICAN REPUBLIC:** Apartado 1742, Santo Domingo. **ECUADOR:** Casilla 09-01-4512, Guayaquil. **EL SALVADOR:** Apartado Postal 401, San Salvador. **ENGLAND:** The Ridgeway, London NW7 1RP. **FIJI:** Box 23, Suva. **FINLAND:** Postbox 68, SF-01301 Vantaa 30. **FRANCE:** B.P. 63, F-92105 Bou!ogne-Billancourt Cedex. **FRENCH GUIANA:** 15 rue Chawari, Cogneau Larivot, 97351 Matoury. **GERMANY:** Postfach 20, W-6251 Selters/Taunus 1. **GHANA:** Box 760, Accra. **GREECE:** P.O. Box 112, GR-322 00 Thiva. **GUADELOUPE:** Monmain, 97180 Sainte Anne. **GUAM 96913:** 143 Jehovah St., Barrigada. **GUATEMALA:** 17 Calle 13-63, Zona 11, 01011 Guatemala. **GUYANA:** 50 Brickdam, Georgetown 16. **HAITI:** Post Box 185, Port-au-Prince. **HAWAII 96819:** 2055 Kam IV Rd., Honolulu. **HONDURAS:** Apartado 147, Tegucigalpa. **HONG KONG:** 4 Kent Road, Kowloon Tong. **HUNGARY:** Pf. 223, H-1425 Budapest. **ICELAND:** P. O. Box 8496, IS-128 Reykjavik. **INDIA:** Post Bag 10, Lonavla, Pune Dis., Mah. 410 401. **IRELAND:** 29A Jamestown Road, Finglas, Dublin 11. **ISRAEL:** P. O. Box 961, 61-009 Tel Aviv. **ITALY:** Via della Bufalotta 1281, I-00138 Rome RM. **JAMAICA:** Box 180, Kingston 10. **JAPAN:** 1271 Nakashinden, Ebina City, Kanagawa Pref., 243-04. **KENYA:** Box 47788, Nairobi. **KOREA, REPUBLIC OF:** Box 33 Pyungtaek P. O., Kyunggido, 450-600. **LEEWARD ISLANDS:** Box 119, St. Johns, Antigua. **LIBERIA:** P. O. Box 10-0380, 1000 Monrovia 10. **LUXEMBOURG:** B. P. 2186, L-1021 Luxembourg, G. D. **MADAGASCAR:** B. P. 511, Antananarivo 101. **MALAYSIA:** 28 Jalan Kampar, Off Jalan Landasan, 41300 Klang, Sel. **MARTINIQUE:** Cours Campeche, Morne Tartenson, 97200 Fort de France. **MAURITIUS:** Box 54, Vacoas. **MEXICO:** Apartado Postal 896, 06002 Mexico, D. F. **MOZAMBIQUE:** Caixa Postal 2600, Maputo. **MYANMAR:** P.O. Box 62, Yangon. **NETHERLANDS:** Noordbargerstraat 77, NL-7812 AA Emmen. **NETHERLANDS ANTILLES:** P.O. Box 4708, Willemstad, Curaçao. **NEW CALEDONIA:** B.P. 787, Nouméa. **NEW ZEALAND:** P.O. Box 142, Manurewa. **NICARAGUA:** Apartado 3587, Managua. **NIGERIA:** P.M.B. 1090, Benin City, Edo State. **NORWAY:** Gaupeveien 24, N-1914 Ytre Enebakk. **PAKISTAN:** 197-A Ahmad Block, New Garden Town, Lahore 54600. **PANAMA:** Apartado 6-2671, Zona 6A, El Dorado. **PAPUA NEW GUINEA:** Box 636, Boroko, N.C.D. **PARAGUAY:** Díaz de Solís 1485 esq. C.A. López, Sajonia, Asunción. **PERU:** Casilla 18-1055, Lima [Av. El Cortijo 329, Monterrico Chico, Lima 33]. **PHILIPPINES, REPUBLIC OF:** P. O. Box 2044, 1099 Manila [186 Roosevelt Ave., San Francisco del Monte, 1105 Quezon City]. **POLAND:** Skr. Poczt. 13, PL-05-830 Nadarzyn. **PORTUGAL:** Apartado 91, P-2766 Estoril Codex [Rua Conde Barão, 511, Alcabideche, P-2765 Estoril]. **PUERTO RICO 00970:** P.O. Box 3980, Guaynabo. **ROMANIA:** Str. Parfumului 22, RO-74121, Bucharest. **RUSSIA:** ul. Tankistov, 4, Solnechnoye, Sestroretzky Rayon, 189640 St. Petersburg. **SENEGAL:** B.P. 3107, Dakar. **SIERRA LEONE, WEST AFRICA:** P. O. Box 136, Freetown. **SLOVAKIA:** V záhradách 33, 811 03 Bratislava. **SOLOMON ISLANDS:** P.O. Box 166, Honiara. **SOUTH AFRICA:** Private Bag X2067, Krugersdorp, 1740. **SPAIN:** Apartado postal 132, E-28850 Torrejón de Ardoz (Madrid). **SRI LANKA, REP. OF:** 62 Layard's Road, Colombo 5. **SURINAME:** P. O. Box 49, Paramaribo. **SWEDEN:** Box 5, S-732 21 Arboga. **SWITZERLAND:** P.O. Box 225, CH-3602 Thun [Ulmenweg 45, Thun]. **TAHITI:** B.P. 518, Papeete. **TAIWAN:** 107 Yun Ho Street, Taipei 10613. **THAILAND:** 69/1 Soi Phasuk, Sukhumvit Rd., Soi 2, Bangkok 10110. **TOGO:** B.P. 4460, Lome. **TRINIDAD AND TOBAGO, REP. OF:** Lower Rapsey Street & Laxmi Lane, Curepe. **UKRAINE:** ul. Olesja, House 11, Apt. 1, 290017 Lviv. **UNITED STATES OF AMERICA:** 25 Columbia Heights, Brooklyn, N.Y. 11201. **URUGUAY:** Francisco Bauzá 3372, 11600 Montevideo. **VENEZUELA:** Apartado 20.364, Caracas, DF 1020A [Av. La Victoria; cruce con 17 de diciembre, La Victoria, Edo. Aragua 2121A]. **WESTERN SAMOA:** P. O. Box 673, Apia. **YUGOSLAVIA, F.R.:** Milorada Mitrovića 4, YU-11 000 Belgrade. **ZAIRE, REP. OF:** B.P. 634, Limete, Kinshasa. **ZAMBIA:** Box 33459, Lusaka 10101. **ZIMBABWE:** 35 Fife Avenue, Harare.